# Now
# What Do
# I Do?

# Now
# What Do
# I Do?

*The Surprising Solution
When Things Go Wrong*

# DR. JOHN TOWNSEND

 **ZONDERVAN®**     ᴀ WORTHY ʙ ᴏ ᴏ ᴋ

**ZONDERVAN**.com/
**AUTHORTRACKER**
*follow your favorite authors*

ZONDERVAN

*Now What Do I Do?*
Copyright © 2010 by John Townsend

Requests for information should be addressed to:

Zondervan, Grand Rapids, Michigan 49530

---

Library of Congress Cataloging-in-Publication Data

Townsend, John Sims, 1952-
    Now what do I do? : the surprising solution when things go wrong / John Townsend.
        p. cm.
      ISBN 978-0-310-32743-1 (hardcover, jacketed)  1.  Problem solving — Religious
    aspects — Christianity.  I. Title.
    BV4599.5.P75T69 2010
    248.8'6 — dc22
                                                                2010000338

# CONTENTS

# The Problem of Having a Problem

"We have to let you go."

It is the sentence that no employee wants to hear. It conveys instability, trouble, and loss. It is not at all welcome. It conveys that we have a problem—one that will affect our lives a great deal. It is also a statement that most of us are hearing, probably more than any other period in our lifetime . . .

My friend Rick, who was a professional in the media sector, got the message recently. He had been successful in his work and had no reason to think he would be out of a job until the global downturn resulted in his company downsizing. With a wife, two teenagers, and a mortgage, he was under pressure to a degree he had never experienced during his career. His family was looking to him to provide for them, as he always had, but he was not able to reassure them he would be able to take care of things. He did not have that invisible shield of employment, a shield that protects us from financial disruption.

Rick went through the same gamut of emotions that any of us would: anxiety, fear, anger, and confusion. He and his wife spent time together talking, and they prayed for answers. But what is most significant is what Rick did *not* do—and you may be surprised. He did not engage in immediate and frantic activities like networking, setting up meetings, and contacting companies to arrange interviews for the next day. He did do those things ultimately, but later on. First, though, Rick took a step back from his situation and engaged in the process that I describe in this book. He had a serious problem, and he began thinking about the best way to address it. In other words, he went through *the steps of problem solving that create the best opportunity for a solution.*

The end result was that, within a few weeks, Rick was employed again, and his family's life has stabilized. He chose a different sector in the IT field, not out of knee-jerk desperation, but as a result of his process of problem solving. That process worked for him. And the problem-solving process you'll read about here will absolutely work for you too. In fact, we almost called this book *The Guaranteed Solution When Things Go Wrong*. But I'm getting ahead of myself.

First let me explain that I didn't take Rick through the process, though I supported him as a friend. Instead, I learned from what he experienced, as well as from the experiences of many people I have dealt with and known over the years. Not all of these people have had career struggles. They experienced a life problem in general, ranging from jobs to relationships to family concerns to health issues. I have been studying people who solve problems well and observing the patterns of the ones who end up the winners. The results of those years of study comprise the DNA of this little book. I have reduced these findings to seven steps for solving a problem, and those steps are for you—not only for your present concern but for anything you encounter, today and for the rest of your life. And I think you'll be surprised. The answers to your problems may actually be where you least expect them . . . as in right in front of you and within you. Just keep reading.

# YOUR PROBLEM REQUIRES AN APPROACH THAT WORKS

As you open up this book, you probably face at least one problem you haven't been able to solve. It may be vaguely troubling, or it may be a present crisis. But what exactly is a problem? Let's understand the term. I define it simply as *a situation in which I want to move from a present state to a desired state, but encounter an obstacle.* Some situation—for example, a relationship issue or a job situation—is going on in my life that I don't like, and I want things to be better. But for any number of reasons, I can't make the change happen easily or quickly. Yes, I do have a problem, but I don't have to stay stuck in it. I can turn to the approach outlined in this book, an approach that works. An approach that you have probably overlooked completely.

Let me explain. If I'm hungry and I want to get lunch at Subway, that's not really a problem. That is simply a need, and every day we spend lots of time and energy meeting all sorts of needs. That is just normal life. Yet none of us should be self-sufficient islands unto ourselves. We all need safety, protection, a livelihood, community, God, and purpose in life. When life works right, we get our needs met, and we meet the needs of others. But if I don't have any money, a car, or directions to Subway, I have a problem. I have to come up with a solution (money, transportation, directions) in order to resolve my problem.

If you are reading this book, you may have a problem in any of the following areas of life:

- Marriage—*You have lost the connection or the trust, or there is an issue with control or hurt.*
- Parenting—*You have a child who is out of control, and you don't seem to know how to reach him.*
- Dating—*You want a good relationship, but haven't been able to find someone who is right for you.*
- Career—*You aren't doing what you are passionate about or are best fit for.*
- Habits and Behaviors—*You want to stop doing some action that isn't good for you, but you continue doing it.*
- Relationships—*You care about someone, but the conflict and distance don't go away.*

Problems, difficulties, and challenges are normal; we all have them. They are simply a part of everyday life. People who say they have no problems are either missing or ignoring some reality. Things happen that shouldn't happen, and such things always will on this earth. Jesus taught that we should accept the reality that, though he wins in the end, "in this world [we] will have trouble. But take heart! I have overcome the world."[1] In this quote, the Greek word for "have trouble" means, literally, "be squashed." That is, your circumstances will press in on you, reducing your freedom to breathe deeply and live life fully. An unsolved problem tends to squash and suffocate us.

And, as I see it, there are two kinds of problems. First are what I call *coping problems*. That is, some issues are truly beyond anything we can do to solve them in our own capacities and strength. They are either just too large or totally out of our control. Maybe you're dealing with a health issue that has no cure, the death of a loved one, an economic shift that renders your job obsolete, or a divorce you did not want. These coping problems are matters of perseverance, support, and prayer. Miracles do happen, and I have experienced them in my life and witnessed them in the lives of others. But beyond that, these are problems that we do our best to adapt to. These problems try our souls yet draw us closer to God and his grace.

The second type of problem is the *curable problem*. They are, as the phrase suggests, fixable. Curable problems are struggles that may be hard, long-term, and very discouraging. But if we commit enough energy and resources to the right steps, those problems have solutions. You may

---

Most of us have curable problems
that we think are actually
coping problems.

---

not see the end in sight. You may have seen no progress or movement in months or years. But there are real, true, and long-lasting solutions.

I believe, however, that *most of us have curable problems that we think are actually coping problems.* That is, we have given up hope that certain situations can truly be different.

The problem has been ongoing for too long, there doesn't seem to be any possible resolution, and it's a large energy drain on us. So something inside us settles for coping: The marriage will always be a C-. The kid will not change; she'll just grow up and leave one day. The dating life will always be empty. I will never have a job that truly fits me. And on and on. *Often, our problem is that we don't know how to deal with our problems.*

If you don't believe in a cure for your problem, though, I understand. In fact, you probably have good reason. Maybe you have waited patiently for someone to change who has no interest in changing. Or maybe you're still trying to conquer a bad habit but you are just out of gas. Or perhaps the effort to keep things going in an unfulfilling job has taken too much out of you. Or you may not have the information or the skills you need to attack the problem you're facing. Or maybe you've decided you can live with the problem and you try not to think about it too much; you just concentrate on other, more fulfilling aspects of life. This is one reason why alienated couples become too (read "unhealthily") involved in parenting, work, or hobbies. Diverting yourself eases the disappointment.

My experience as both a psychologist and business coach has led me in a different direction than this sad turn. Things will never be perfect in life, but I have observed that if people will follow the basic problem-solving approach in this book, their life circumstances can be much, much better than they are today. God has not left us to simply cope in life and hope for a better day in the by and by. He wants to guide, teach, empower, and grow us up. This following seven-step approach is designed to give you success over whatever is getting in your way in life. It's the approach Rick took when, unexpectedly laid off, he turned that problem into an opportunity. And I know you can do the same.

## THE VIEW FROM A CELL PHONE

One way to understand the following approach to problem solving is to think about the one item most of us can't leave home without: our cell phone. We are almost surgically connected to our mobile communication devices. We stay in touch with the people who matter to us via voice, text, and e-mail. It is our link to the universe. It's hard to remember when we had no cell with us, and we had to go home, to the office, or to a pay phone to make a call. But back to my point.

You have almost certainly had your cell break down on you. For whatever reason, you couldn't send or receive, and you were alone in the world, cut off from all contact—or at least that's how it felt. When our cell phone stops working, though, most of us don't simply put it back in our pocket and say, "Oh well, I'll take a look when I have time." Instead, life stops right then and there. You end the conversation you are having at the restaurant, or you excuse yourself from the business meeting. You may even pull the car over to the side of the road. My teenagers tell me that when they don't have access to their cells, they feel anxious inside, as if they're missing out on life.

When that cell phone does go down, most people have their own personal system for diagnosing the problems. Whether or not you have consciously thought about it—and you have probably not written it down—you have a system. It may be effective or useless, but there is a protocol you go through. Normally, the best approach is something like this:

I. Press the "Send" button a few more times.
2. Check the number of bars to see what kind of range you have.
3. Check the battery.
4. Remove the battery and put it back in.
5. If you're a techie, check to see if there is a software conflict.
6. Take your phone to a techie friend.
7. Go online and try to solve the problem.
8. Drive to the cellular store and take it to the repair department.

These cell-phone repair steps have an order and a meaning to them. The approach is somewhere in the realm of being pretty well thought-out. However, there are some people whose approach is far less well thought-out. They shake the device up and down. They press all the buttons randomly. They bang the phone on the table to loosen up whatever may have disconnected. It's a system, though a poor one.

Here is my point. You have a problem, more bothersome than serious, but a problem all the same. Just as you have an established procedure for when your cell phone breaks down, you also have one for problems you encounter in life. Whether the issue is job, relationship, family, parenting, marriage, or personal habits, there is a way you "do problems." Below are some of the less helpful systems we tend to use, often simply because we are comfortable with them or we haven't sat down and intentionally thought about a good way to look at problems:

**Learned helplessness:** "I may as well give up now. This one is beyond me. I lose."

**Feeling overwhelmed:** "I have no idea where to start. The situation is too big, too scary, and too complicated for me."

**The last straw:** "I have too much on my plate already. I could handle this if it were the only thing going on in my life, but it's one of a thousand things."

**Powering through:** "I'll put more and more energy into beating my head against this problem, doing nothing new, but hoping my head is harder than the problem." (It usually isn't.)

**Overanalyzing:** "I'll study and research this, I'll talk to people about this all the way to the DNA level, but I will not take any action steps."

**Avoidance:** "If I do something else, maybe the problem will go away."

**Cries for rescue:** "I need someone to do this for me, but who will help me?"

**Blame:** "I didn't cause this problem, so maybe I can find who is at fault and get them to fix it. Until then, I'll live with the misery."

Perhaps you identify with one of these styles more than the others; I have certainly done my share of them. The point is, each of us already has an approach to problem solving, but it probably isn't all that effective or helpful. When you learn to deal effectively with a problem, though, you will find that *less energy can create more results.* So it is to your advantage to have the most effective approach in place, to be ready for whatever you find yourself facing. That is the purpose of this book: to give you a big-picture yet simple way to address and attack any problem. This book will provide an overall system for whatever you encounter today.

Actually, we have learned much about problem solving from the field of mathematics, from puzzles and Rubik's cubes to complex algorithms developed to solve world hunger. For many years people have been using numbers to solve difficult issues, and today computers play a large part in these exercises. Math experts are trained to expect problems, understand problems, spend a great deal of time thinking about problems, and, ultimately, solve problems. Mathematicians don't dislike problems. In fact, problems are the air they breathe. Businesspeople, in the

———

Your relationships, your emotions,
and your character play
a significant role in how
you solve problems.

———

same vein, expect problems. In fact, if there are no problems, they look for them, because the apparent absence of problems generally means they are missing something important.

Interestingly, just like books about math and finance, now books about relational issues and social problems include strategies and approaches. These books use systematic thinking to get people somewhere they want to go. The authors have done their own research and developed their own theories, most of which include such basic aspects as clearly defining the problem, brainstorming answers, deciding on a course to take, and executing the idea.[2]

The uniqueness of this book—which does include the researched parts of solutions that any good process has—is the assumption it makes. This material assumes that *your relationships, your emotions, and your character play a significant role in how you solve problems.* That is, problem solving goes beyond good sense and logic. You also must apply much more to the issue: you must apply yourself as a person—body, soul, mind, and strength—if you are to solve problems well.

And the approach you're going to read about has a very high probability of working well for you. Even if you've lost track of how many times you've started trying to solve a problem and, way before you even created an action plan, became overwhelmed and given up . . . Even if anxiety has kept you from being creative . . . Even if you haven't known how to identify or use the resources at your disposal . . . And even if, not knowing who to ask for help, you've found yourself trying to go it alone. This book will provide a simple, doable, surefire seven-step process that will clarify how you can better understand your problem and, in a short period of time, make significant progress toward solving it.

Also, remember that you are not alone in this. God understands and wants to be involved in your pursuit of solutions. God is no stranger to problems—or to solving them. One of his problems, for example, was a people alienated from his love and care. He did not cause or create this problem that pained him greatly, yet he went to great lengths to solve that problem: "God was reconciling the world to himself in Christ."[3] And every day he continues this work of reconciliation. He will also work *with* you and *in* you to solve whatever your problem is . . . in his way and his time.

So maybe you don't have a great track record as a problem solver—yet. Maybe you're not confident about your ability to evaluate and plan a course of action. Well, this is a new day. You can definitely learn from the ideas in this book how to successfully solve whatever problems come your way.

## STEP 1:

# Feel What You Feel

*Feeling and longing are the motive forces behind
all human endeavor and human creations.*
*—Albert Einstein*

The first thing you should do when you encounter a problem that stymies you may not be what you expect . . .

When you first find yourself dealing with a situation that will take some work and effort, *feel what you are feeling*. Before trying to get some distance in order to analyze the issues, allow yourself to feel your emotions in the moment.

We are all emotional beings. Whether we are always aware of them or not, we have feelings. You are feeling something right now while you are reading this chapter. It may be slight, perhaps a little anticipation or interest;

hopefully it's not boredom. Like an underlying current in the ocean, your feelings are alive and well, whether below or above the surface. And it benefits you to become aware of what your emotional state is whenever you run into a roadblock.

Most of the time, obviously, the feelings that come with roadblocks are more negative than positive. You may feel anxiety, anger, fear, or sadness, for example. Problems, being essentially negative in nature, bring about the darker feelings in us.

Suppose you are single and can't find a decent dating relationship. You've tried the normal circles: friends' referrals, online sites, church singles groups, and the like, but you can't find anyone you really connect with on any sort of a satisfying and meaningful level. If that's the case, it is pretty normal to feel frustration, emptiness, and discouragement. To feel nothing at all would mean that something in you is frozen, and to feel happy wouldn't match the reality you are dealing with. Clearly, your feelings mirror your situation, your problem.

# FEELINGS: A HELP, NOT A HINDRANCE

This first step in problem solving may not make any sense at all to you. You might be thinking, *What good would feeling what I'm feeling do? I'll just end up wallowing in self-pity, freezing up in anxiety, or pounding my head against the desk. To solve a problem, I need to think clearly. Aren't my feelings the last thing I need to be paying attention to?* It certainly does seem that in a time of trouble, you need a plan, decisiveness, and action. If you are a commercial pilot and you have just lost an engine, you need to be much more focused on your emergency protocols and your hand–eye coordination than your emotions.

You may also be concerned that your feelings will either guide you into a rash decision or make you act in an out-of-control manner. How many times have you heard someone mention a sexual indiscretion regretfully, saying, "The feelings got out of hand"? It is true that feelings can be intense and powerful. But my experience of emotions is that when they are balanced by good judgment and values, and when we are around good and safe people, our feelings won't rule our lives. So don't shut them down and don't let them take over. Above all, don't be afraid of emotions. Your feelings are your servants, not your masters.

Aside from urgent situations like the one you as the pilot found yourself in, there are three very good reasons for feeling what you feel when you are faced with a difficulty.

---

Your feelings are your servants,
not your masters.

---

**You need emotions for the information they provide.** Feelings, whether they be happy or sad, have purposes, meaning, and reasons for existing. Feelings don't simply exist to make life interesting or make you miserable. In fact, feelings are a valuable source of information for you. If you pay attention to them, you will learn a lot that can help you crunch your problem.

Let's understand a little about what feelings tell us. I have written about this before in a leadership context,[1] but the message applies to us all: emotions are a signal. They tell us that something is going on that we need to pay attention to. Feelings are part of how God helps us look within ourselves: "Search me, O God, and know my heart; test me and know my anxious thoughts."[2]

For example, *anxiety* is an emotion associated with concern, fear, or panic. The message of anxiety is that *there is some danger to avoid or be aware of*. Anxiety directs us to look around for dangers. The danger may, for instance, be a toxic person telling you he is safe for you. It may be an investment that looks great, but you don't like some of the deal points. It may be the awareness that you are drinking too much and cannot control yourself.

Do you see how valuable anxiety is when you are in the moment with your problem, whatever that problem may be? Here is an example. I was coaching a man who was your basic "take the hill" executive. He loved the action of business, the strategies, and the hunt. And he was very good at what he did. But he often made commitments to people and projects that weren't good for him. If he liked what he saw, he went for it. And he found himself not getting ahead in his career because he kept having to recover from bad deals and interactions with the wrong people. So what was his problem? He was not where he wanted to be at his age and stage in life.

Once I saw the pattern, I told him, "You don't like to feel anxiety, because it doesn't fit your self concept of a banzai, go-for-it guy." He reluctantly agreed. I explained, "Your enthusiasm and action are great, but you aren't checking for anxiety. When you hear a pitch or talk to a

---

Your anger doesn't mean you are
a bad, violent, or out-of-control
person. Anger simply says that
you need to solve a problem
of some sort.

---

candidate for a position with you, take a moment to see if you feel any anxiety." When my client combined sensitivity to his anxiety level with his banzai nature, he eventually began to understand that some people and some deals were too good to be true. The lack of integrity, truthfulness, or soundness caused an anxious vibe within him. He didn't enjoy feeling that, but he used the information those feelings provided. Gradually, his career took on the upward trajectory he had been wanting. (Anxiety is such a critical aspect to problem solving that it reappears at its own step, number 4. We will go into depth on anxiety and fear there.)

*Anger* is another helpful feeling. Your anger doesn't mean you are a bad, violent, or out-of-control person. Anger simply says that you need to solve a problem of some sort. It is an emotion that, instead of moving us to avoid something like anxiety does, moves us to address and confront something. Anger helps people take action against injustice and poverty. It motivates us to confront someone who is being destructive. It helps us determine not to repeat the same mistakes we've already made.

Suppose your problem is a rebellious teen, whose disrespectful words and conduct are wreaking havoc in your home. It is common for parents to suppress their anger at the adolescent, for fear of escalating that negative emotion and to avoid having two or three angry people lock horns. So instead these parents try to be reasonable, mature, and patient, all good qualities for moms and dads to have. However, we parents need to understand that bad behavior that disrupts a loving home *should* make us angry. Anger says, "Enough! We have to confront this directly, with conversations, consequences, a counselor, or some plan. I can't have this anymore." That doesn't mean that you spill your anger onto your teen, an act that really could make things get out of control. So you may need to talk about your anger and share that emotion with someone safe in your life. The point here is, learn from your anger and use it.

**You need emotions to connect you to supportive people.** Emotions are great connectors. When you are in love, there is a person on the receiving end. Often when you are frustrated, you are disturbed by another person's bad behavior. Emotions do keep us relating to one another in deep and meaningful ways. And if there ever is a time when you need that kind of connection, it's when you encounter a life problem.

Once I was working with a father who felt an enormous responsibility to be strong and never show weakness. He wanted to keep his family safe, happy, and secure. Even when his business was struggling, he wanted to protect his family, so even though his kids were teens and fully capable of dealing with financial realities, he kept quiet. Over time, he distanced himself from his wife and kids. He didn't know how to convey the anxiety and insecurity he felt to the ones who loved him, so he just shut down and would hardly talk. His family missed him, but they didn't know what to do.

I listened to the whole family for a while, and then I said, "I'm concerned that you're going to have some sort of a breakdown if you don't let your family in." His eyes filled with tears, and he said in a surprised voice, "I think I might be breaking down now." I watched his wife and kids move toward him and support his sadness and his sense of being overwhelmed. They loved him, comforted him, and connected on a deeper level with him than ever before. His wife said, "I want you to always let me know when you feel this way."

This man had a long road ahead of him to put his professional life back together. But, fueled by the grace of the people he loved, he was able to better persevere. Just as this man learned to do, you need to use your feelings to gain the support and love of those who will help you deal with, if not solve, your problem. (In the next chapter we will deal more fully with the importance of others in crunching problems.)

**When you ignore your emotions, you deplete energy you need to solve your problem.** Attempting to "unfeel" whatever you feel is a huge drain on your energy, and that effort can siphon off the power you need to crunch your problem. Trying not to feel what you feel is like telling an earthquake, "Just stop that!"

Have you ever said any of these statements?

- Forget the feeling and get moving.
- I need to stop feeling this.
- I need to just get busy, and the feelings will go away.
- I'll tell myself the truth, and that will fix the feeling.

While there are times when we do need to get moving (remember the pilot!), this approach will never work for the long term. God meant feelings to help us search, with himself and with one another, for truth in our innermost parts: "The purposes of a man's heart are deep waters, but a man of understanding draws them out."[3]

The Hebrew word for "heart" means "inner person," which includes passions, emotions, and values. All emotions are meant to be expressed and "drawn out." That is the nature of feelings. So we are acting counter to God's design when we pretend our feelings don't exist.

Furthermore, any attempts to not feel what you feel, or to ignore your feelings, or to simply deny that you have feelings will take energy to maintain. That is why, in counseling, when a person who has stayed in her head all her life and not dealt with her heart finally senses she is safe enough to feel things, that experience can be overwhelming. The years of emotions catch up with her, and she has to go through a season of feeling what she never allowed herself to feel. It's just better to keep short accounts on feelings and save the energy for the problem you are facing.

## BEFRIENDING YOUR FEELINGS

Several skills will enable you to maximize the help your emotions can offer as you deal with problems. Here are some practical steps to follow.

**Add emotions to your vocabulary.** What you can talk about, you can better feel and understand. When we have a word for a feeling, we give that feeling permission to be experienced and talked about. One of the jobs of parenting is to put words to experiences for one's children. For example, "You didn't play a lot at the soccer game today. You must be sad, and I am sad for you. Come on, let's get a yogurt and talk about what you learned about soccer." Without a word to use for her feelings, your child is left with some vague "down" experience inside her head and nowhere to go with it. With words, though, she can talk to Mom, know that she has expressed herself, feel understood by Mom, and get on with solving her problem.

To put this step into action, find a list of feelings online or through the American Psychological Association that categorizes emotions, with various shadings and nuances, from positive to negative. For example, *anxious* and *terrified* are cousins, but they are different in what they convey. Review the list and try to use three "feelings" words every day in a conversation with a person who understands feelings. Do this until you have gone through the list. After this exercise, you will be surprised at how much more comfortable you are with your feelings.

**Spend five minutes a day alone thinking about your problem. During that time, be open to your emotions. List whatever feelings you notice.** Most of us aren't even aware of what we feel because we are frantically busy, we are never alone, or we are a little afraid of what is down inside. But bite the bullet and open up some RAM space in your mind for your feelings. Sit down at your desk or the kitchen table when no one is around. Turn off your cell phone and think to yourself, *I have a medical issue*, or *I can't stop overeating*, or *I don't have a passion for my job*, or *I am falling out of love and I don't want to.*

This kind of simple focus is a message to your feelings: *It's OK. I want to hear from you.* You may be surprised by your feelings, and that's all right. You are on a hunt for information.

One woman I worked with was in the last category listed above: she didn't feel love for her husband. When she allowed herself to identify her true feeling about this situation, it was relief. "This is weird," she said, "and I feel a little guilty. Shouldn't I be feeling bad about not feeling love for my husband?" I told her, "Not unless you've been pretending you felt something else for him and have been disconnected from yourself for years." She understood that, for that is exactly what she had been doing. And her awareness of her pretending helped her reenter the marriage and learn to authentically love again.

**Record the information that you learn about the problem from your feelings.** Remember, your feelings are telling you something about yourself. Listen to your feelings and note what you learn. You will find value there, as these examples illustrate:

*I feel helpless in my marriage: I can't change how he behaves toward me.* Helplessness tells you that you don't feel you have choices. It suggests a sense of powerlessness and impotence, but that unfortunate feeling can lead to one of two positive solutions. First, you may be trying to control something you can have no control over, such

Your feelings are telling you
something about yourself. Listen to
them and note what you learn.
You will find value there.

as your spouse's feelings or behaviors. If that is the case, give it up. You have nothing to gain. Your efforts to control the uncontrollable will only make the situation worse, even if you feel you are in the right. Second, you may be neglecting to control something you can and should take charge of.

When people feel helpless in a relationship, they often give a great deal of power to the other person, and it really helps the relationship for that person to take back the power. You may, for instance, decide you need to learn to make your own choices in life—choices that move you closer to your goals—whether or not he understands or fully supports you. Or you may decide you will not allow him to speak to you in a certain way, and when he does, you leave the room. These examples drive home the point that your feelings are your friend, and they can help you make choices and solve your problem.

*I am frustrated with my job. My boss expects too much of me and doesn't support me.* I recently talked to a man at a leadership conference who works for an energy company, and apparently his boss is pretty clueless. When he expressed his frustration to me, we used that frustration to get him moving down a road he needed to travel. He wanted to be productive and successful in his position, but he got no good direction or clarity from his boss. So the plan we worked out was to tell his boss, "I want to make you successful. I want to help you meet your goals. But I need more clarity from you. Can we meet and come up with some plans?" The conversation didn't immediately solve the entire problem, but it was a good start.

The point I am trying to make is a simple one: feelings are not just window dressing in life. They are vital to understanding the nature of your problem so that you are more informed, and they are good for your well-being. What is more, your emotions are a tool that will help you solve your problem. So embrace your feelings; pay attention to them and learn from them. You will be the better for it.

# Get with the Right People

*Consult your friend on all things, especially on
those which respect yourself. His counsel may then
be useful where your own self-love might
impair your judgment.*
—*Seneca (5 BC–65 AD)*

It is almost a given that, when faced with a troubling problem, most of us begin to shut down and "go inside." Whether it be a long-term and difficult marriage issue, a parenting struggle, or a job conflict, we tend to withdraw for some period of time. We don't reach out to others; we direct our energy internally. There are good reasons for this pattern: your system is focusing, marshalling its resources and defenses, and paying attention to solving the problem at hand.

Women who are in labor, for example, are extremely focused on the profound levels of difficulty, pain, importance, meaning, and joy they are experiencing in that most wondrous aspect of life. Or consider a three-year-old who falls down unexpectedly and is silent for several seconds, almost in shock, but then draws a huge breath and begins to scream. Or, similarly, when you are in the office and read an e-mail that has bad financial news, you most likely shut your door, take a deep breath, reread the message, and sit alone for a moment, pondering what you just read.

A lot of good can happen when you are facing a problem and take time to reflect. As we observed in the previous chapter, those minutes can be a valuable time to feel your emotions and learn from them. And it can be a time when you begin to think through the problem and better understand its nature, so that you can put together a plan. This "cave time," however, should have limits. You need to connect with others, to reach out and pull in support from the right relationships in your life and from those people who know how to solve big problems and who will walk with you. Certainly God is the primary One who forges the way for us, leads us, and guides us. We are to trust and follow him instead of going it alone. Also, we are designed to help and be helped by one another: "Two are better than one, because they have a good return for their work: If one falls down, his friend can help him up. But pity the man who falls and has no one to help him up!"[1]

## THE RELATIONSHIP FACTOR

When we fall down, it is increasingly clear to us that we really do need people. We are created for relationship. We

---

Being known and cared about by others is not a luxury or an enhancement to life; it is a necessity.

---

are to live in community. We are to live in connection with people who both know us well and are good for us. In fact, *being known and cared about by others is not a luxury or an enhancement to life; it is a necessity.* Without the ability to trust and have others "inside" you, you are likely to struggle with relationships, health, career, and even emotional illness. In terms of problem solving, the same is true: when you have a problem you can't solve immediately, you must have other individuals in place ready to help you.

I can't overemphasize this second key to problem solving. When you are facing a challenge, you need to give up the Lone Ranger stance and make sure you have others on your team. People who crunch problems do so much better in relationship. People who are isolated and don't let others in on their situation—they risk being crunched themselves.

My friend Kevin recently encountered a perfect storm of problems. He and his fiancée went on the skids. The IRS audited his company and froze his assets. And he experienced some severe health problems that landed him in the hospital. I had known Kevin for some time, and I knew him to be one of those people who is more comfortable giving than receiving. He is a great leader and provider, but he does not have a good track record of asking for help and support. Doing so makes him feel weak and vulnerable. In the family he came from, alcoholism and incompetent parents created chaos for him, so he quickly learned to be the strong one, the achiever, the caretaker—and he did not turn away from this stance for many years. After all, it worked for him . . . to a point. He continued to face marriage, parenting, and career issues that stemmed from his inability to let anyone close.

Fortunately—and before the perfect storm hit— Kevin had become aware that his *self-sufficiency was not a virtue, but a weakness;* that his self-sufficiency was nothing to be proud of, but actually a hindrance to his becoming a better and more successful person. As a result, he realized he needed other people, so he joined a small group that was designed for support and personal growth. For a while, Kevin tried to be the helper for the other members, but, in a kind but firm manner, they put a stop to that, telling him, "Knock it off, hero. We want you to let us into your life." So, over time, Kevin stepped out of his comfort zone and allowed the group to know him, care about him, and support him.

As Kevin became comfortable with these relationships, he found himself having e-mail, phone calls, and face-to-face meetings with members of his group. His life began to be intertwined with their lives. As I look back, I realize that, in some way, without being aware of it, Kevin was building a foundation for what he was to encounter.

When the relational/financial/medical storm hit, Kevin knew what to do. He called his group friends and said, "I'm in trouble. I don't have anything to offer anyone. I need help." This was a counterintuitive move for him—and not at all a comfortable step for him to take.

---

Two contributions that people bring to other people are connection and reality.

---

But Kevin was getting out of the cave of his isolation and moving into the light of human need and vulnerability. And the miracle happened. The group rallied in a way that was very moving. They took turns calling Kevin and visiting him daily. They had prayer times for him. They offered advice and practical help. It wasn't easy for Kevin to receive all this. He felt unworthy, and he worried that he was a lot of trouble for his friends. The group told him, "Suck it up! It's your turn to be the person who gets help!"

As of the time of this writing, Kevin is not yet out of the woods. His circumstances are still difficult, but he will tell you, as he told me, that he is much farther along in solving his issues than he would have been had he resorted to his natural tendency to live life in the cave.

## BREAKING DOWN THE ELEMENTS

Let's look at the value of relationship for successful problem solving. Follow the example of a pharmaceutical researcher who combines the correct chemicals to cure a medical condition. Think about people as a chemical ingredient that helps cure the disease of thorny problems. What do we human beings actually provide one another that helps in those situations?

I have written extensively on this subject elsewhere,[2] but I'll offer a quick-and-dirty summary. Two basic umbrella contributions that people bring to other people are connection and reality.

**Connection.** I use this word to refer to "a transfer of intangibles from one person to another." These intangibles are the fuel of life for us even though we cannot see them. Connection provides you with love, comfort, support, empathy, and encouragement. When you are deeply connected to others, you can navigate the storms of life much more easily even if your friends don't give you advice or answers.

Just being with people who are "for" you, who understand you, and who will walk with you has tremendous value. Their presence in your life enables you to have the energy, motivation, clarity, creativity, and strength you need to crunch your problem. It sounds counterintuitive to people who are unfamiliar with relationship dynamics, but it is simply true. People who allow safe people into their lives have a better quality of life and, being well connected with others, they are more competent problem-solvers.

A friend of mine called me about a problem he was having with his adult son. The son, who had a drug problem, was refusing any help from his dad, and Dad was understandably distraught. It is a helpless feeling to be unable to do anything for your child when that "child" is an emancipated adult who can put himself beyond the reach of your help. The dad and I discussed some ideas and strategies for how to approach the son. At the end of the phone call, my friend said, "I already knew most of the answers we talked about, but what helped most was that you understand. I know I'm not alone with all this." Connection may be intangible and invisible, but so is a molecule of an antibiotic. And both are powerful aids in times of trouble.

**Reality.** At the same time that you and I need connection with one another, we also need the reality that comes with relationship. That is, you need to get with people who know you and who know something about the problem. Reality has to do with advice, wisdom, expertise, experience, and competence. It can be about who you are as a person and about your own tendencies and reactions; it can be about the subject matter you are facing right now. Reality has to do with what is and what do I do now.

We all have a tendency to think, *My problem is unique. No one has faced this in the same way that I am having to face it.* It is certainly true that nothing is exactly the same for two different people. We are all like snowflakes in our uniqueness and, therefore, in the uniqueness of our experiences. But being snowflakes doesn't mean that we can't all become snowmen using the same principles. Your situation and problem have been faced, generally speaking, by lots of people who have come before you in history, and there is a finite number of ways we can struggle. There are lots of problems, but not an infinite number of them. People can provide you with the perspectives and solutions that can go a long way for you.

---

People can provide you
with the perspectives and
solutions that can go
a long way for you.

---

I was talking to a woman whose boyfriend had strayed from her and lied about another relationship he was having. This experience was devastating, because she was very attached to him and had thought he was The One. Her kids also loved this man, and she didn't know how to approach the matter with them. It was a heartbreaking problem for this woman, and one in which she had no experience. She had been widowed and soon thereafter gotten connected to this man. So all the complexities of dating, betrayal, healing, forgiveness, and blended family dynamics were a new and unfamiliar world for her.

I was at an airport between flights when she called me. I asked her how urgent things were. Did she want to wait until I was home next week to talk longer? Did she want me to refer her to a therapist I would recommend for that situation? Or did she want to talk now, in the few minutes we had until my flight left? She opted for the latter.

Within thirty minutes, we had unraveled the problem and put together a basic and workable game plan. She was to make a clear and clean break with the man, who had shown no signs of wanting to give up the other woman. She was to tell the kids in age-appropriate language—and without the gory details—that he wouldn't be coming around anymore. She was to get into a support group with people who were better versed in the singles world and could mentor her. She was to talk to these people before she started another relationship and run the new guy past them. And she was not to bring her kids into connection with a man she was dating until she was in the engagement phase (my personal counseling rule to protect kids). All of these suggestions formed a healthy path for her to walk.

My friend was surprised we got so much reality handled in one phone call. She had thought it would take weeks and weeks of conversation. I said, "Sometimes it does, but you were very open and nondefensive. You

---

Get with people who have information and reality that will help you.

---

wanted reality. And we were talking about something that lots of people I have worked with have dealt with for a long time. You are a financial expert yourself [she was CFO of an organization]. If I had called you with an investment or tax question, how complicated would it have been for you to help me?" She said, "Maybe thirty minutes if you gave me the right information."

She got it, and I hope you get it. Get with people who have information and reality that will help you. You may have to do a lot on your own, and there are few, if any, magical answers. But reality will get you on the right path for solving your problem.

## THE RIGHT PEOPLE AND THE RIGHT WAY TO UTILIZE THEM

You may at this point be thinking, *I understand. I need to talk to my friends instead of worrying about my problem all by myself. OK. Now what's the next step?* If these are your thoughts, slow down and think a little more deeply here. There is more to this topic than just having friends. You need the right kind of relationships. Are you sure you have them at this point? You also need to structure these relationships in a particular way, and you may not currently be doing that. Here are my recommendations.

**Character.** You need people who have the right sort of character. Their insides need to be the right insides. Not anyone will do. There are friends, which we all have. And then there are friends who have good character. Your season of problem crunching requires people who are able to give you significant connection and significant reality. People of character.

And I define *character* as something more than personal integrity, honesty, and authenticity. It is *having the abilities required to meet the demands of reality*, a definition Henry Cloud and I use in many of our writings.[3] Life makes lots of demands on us: financial, relational, parenting, marriage, health, dating, and career, for starters. Think for a moment about the problems you face. Most likely, they are mentioned in the list above. To meet those demands, we need certain skills and abilities. Only then will we be able to meet life's obligations.

So it simply makes sense that your friends make a deep emotional attachment with you; that is, they connect on meaningful levels and "get" you. They should be honest and clear about who they are, and they should possess good boundaries. They also need to know how to deal with and make the best of negative realities, failures, and struggles. And they should know what their gifts and talents are and how to invest them in their friendship with you. These abilities mean your friends have something to give you that will help you navigate the currently choppy waters of your life.

Here is the point: choose as your friends-in-hard-times people who have the equipment, the internal stuff, that will help you. This doesn't mean you should necessarily leave or dismiss your current friends. We all have lots of relationships for lots of reasons. Don't ignore the workaholic, the casual friend, or the party person—unless you are recovering from alcoholism! All these people have their place in your life. But do conduct a dedicated search for a few right people to be friends when you're in need.

**Utilizing vs. Using.** You need to utilize—not use—your friends: benefit from their strong character and ask for their advice, their help, their support, and their wisdom. Don't shirk from telling your friends what you need. Good friends appreciate that. Sometimes we are afraid of *utilizing* our friends because we think we are *using* them. But these two actions are worlds apart. When we use people, we take advantage of the relationship and exploit them for our gain.

For example, a friend of mine who is very well networked in the business community was suggesting names of people for me to contact when I was working on a business project. He looked at his list and got to one name and said, "Don't call this guy. He takes a lot more than he gives, and everyone knows it." I asked what he meant, and he said, "Whenever I talk to him, he wants to know what

I can do for him, what sorts of deals and projects I can involve him with. He doesn't care about me, and he rarely asks how I am doing." But to utilize someone is a different matter. Rather than exploiting that person, you enjoy a give-and-take relationship. You care about each other's lives, victories, and sorrows. You freely ask each other for help, support, suggestions, and wisdom. A friendship like that is what enriches our lives.

A friend of mine was hit hard by the economic downturn of 2008. Her husband's profession took a big hit, and she lost her part-time job. She decided that, with little to lose at this point, she should try to find a job doing something she enjoyed. Nothing from nothing leaves nothing. Her "Now what do I do?" challenge was to find a way to make money doing something she loves. She enrolled in my job-coaching program and immersed herself in finding her passion. It ended up that she loved public speaking, and she had engaging, informative material to share. But she didn't know where to start in terms of getting opportunities to speak. She didn't have the necessary connections to start speaking at schools, churches, business meetings, Rotary clubs, etc. When she realized this was where she got stuck, I suggested that she make a list of people she knew who might have the right connections and ask them to give her names and contact information. This step was a little hard for her, because she didn't want people to think she was using them. I explained to her, "You have paid your dues. These people know that you care about them, and you have done things to help them grow and make it in life as well. Take a risk and ask them. See how they respond."

Still feeling a little fear and trepidation, she made the calls—and her friends were happy to give her the information she asked for. They even offered to help more. She was a little surprised by that, but their reaction helped her understand the difference between using and utilizing people.

Let me ask you a question: when someone who genuinely cares about your well-being asks you a favor, do you feel taken advantage of, or are you glad to help? If you are reasonably healthy, you answered that you are glad to help. Yes, friends should be utilized.

**Structure.** When a problem is knotty enough for you to be reading this book, it means you have tried a lot of things up to this point and have not gotten the results you want. It also means that you may not be utilizing your friends as effectively as you can. A lot of life and many problem-solving opportunities require making the best use of time, energy, and focus. And sometimes we need to add structure to our relationships if we are to get the most help for a difficult situation.

When you have found a few "right" people, you may want to ask them if you can meet with or talk to them on a regular basis. That request may mean making several different contacts with several different people during a week. Or, if possible, it might mean getting those people together in the same room at the same time to help you in a more synergetic way. That is more difficult logistically, but it can be extremely helpful.

My pastor asked me to join a board specifically created to address media development at my church. He recruited people with different experience in film, art, media, theology, business, and finance. We met for a prescribed period of time, and then the project ended. But it was a great experience to see the members interact from our different perspectives as we zeroed in on the task.

In your case, you may have some great people, and you can simply meet or talk with them about your job, relationship, or financial issue. Increasingly, though, I am finding that this doesn't work for me—or for most people. How many times have you played voice-mail tag, in between both your meetings, with someone you want

---

Sometimes we need to add
structure to our relationships if
we are to get the most help for a
difficult situation.

---

to talk to? So I recommend that you ask a few people for regular talks—say, once a week for thirty minutes apiece, for a month or so. If people know what commitment you are asking for, and especially if it is for a limited number of weeks, they are much more likely to think, "Shelley is a friend for life, but this project involves just four meetings. I can do this with her."

Add structure to your relationships with the right people, and you add the power of support and wisdom. I will often have short phone meetings with people who need some quick advice. We will calendar the time, and the person will develop the agenda ahead of time, determining in advance what they want to discuss and identifying the questions they have. While these calls are friendly, they are not social calls. When we make contact, I will simply say, "OK, what do you want to work on?" and we'll dive right in.

It is amazing what focus will do to solve a problem.

# Build a Strong Fence

*Science is organized knowledge.*
*Wisdom is organized life.*
—*Immanuel Kant*

For many years, I have been cohosting a nationally syndicated daily call-in radio show. This counseling program is called *New Life Live*, and we have dealt with literally thousands of "Now what do I do?" situations. I'm sure there are issues we haven't heard about from people, but the program has definitely covered a lot of ground!

Part of every conversation involves training time that, in a way, helps the callers clarify why they are calling. If you've heard the show, you know our approach. It goes like this:

"Hi, Bob in Indiana. How are you?"

"Good. How are you guys?"

"We're fine. How can we help?"

"Well, I have a situation with my mom. When she comes over, she is really critical of my wife and how she keeps the house and disciplines our kids." Bob then provides more information as context for his call.

"Sounds like it's hard to be between your wife and your mom. What's your question?"

"Yeah, it's really hard. I don't want to hurt my mom's feelings, but I don't want to let my wife down either."

"That is a struggle, Bob. So what's your question?"

"I really care about both of them, you know. My wife says I'm not putting her first."

"We understand. So what's your question?"

"My question? Well, I guess it's 'How do I talk to Mom without hurting her feelings?'"

"Great question. A lot of people have this struggle. Here are some ideas ..."

We human beings don't naturally have the ability to "ask the question" when we are faced with a tough problem. We tend to ruminate, worry, obsess, discuss the problem at length, and analyze it to death. All that's necessary and important, because the more you understand an issue, the better off you are when it comes to finding a solution. But at some point you do need to ask the question.

As accomplished problem-solvers know and appreciate, *it is critical to define and set parameters around your problem.* You need to know where your problem begins and where

---

You need to know where your problem begins and ends. This is a simple but essential matter of clarity.

---

it ends. This is a simple but essential matter of clarity. In fact, you'll be surprised at how far along you get toward resolving an issue when you take this step. Definition and clarity always help us gain traction in our problem solving, and we shouldn't be surprised since "God is not a God of disorder but of peace."[1]

## WHAT PARAMETERS ACCOMPLISH

There are two practical reasons why clearly defining your problem is a key step toward solving it. First, as much as possible, *you want to integrate your solution into your normal life rather than let the problem redefine your life.* Problems are disruptive enough. They worry us, they distract us, they interfere with our dreams and goals, and they take a lot of our energy. Yes, problems can greatly affect your life, but letting them define your life is giving them entirely too much power. Don't let your problems derail everything else that matters to you. Certainly—and sadly—there are exceptions to this: a serious illness or a crisis with a child, for example, can tend to redefine life, at least temporarily. When a friend of mine got cancer, her husband, family, friends, and church rallied around her in an unusually supportive way for a year. Thankfully, she is fine now, but for a very scary year, nothing mattered except her condition and her treatment.

Except in extreme situations like these, however, it is best to define your problem as specifically as possible. Set parameters on exactly what the problem is, and what it isn't, so that you can continue those life activities—your relationships, your career, your interests—that are good, healthy, and meaningful. Parameters help you say, *I've done all I can do about this problem today, and it's time to return to normal life.* If we don't set parameters, it is too easy to drop out of life and concentrate only on the issue: *I can't enjoy life until I have the right job or the right dating relationship; I can't be close to my spouse until we have resolved all our differences;* or *I can't be happy unless my kids have no struggles.* Parameters protect you from this life-draining thinking.

Second, in addition to keeping problems from taking over our life, *parameters teach us to be diligent and patient with our problems.* They help us learn to sow seeds of health and good things and to wait for the harvest. The happiest and healthiest people in the world understand this secret of delayed gratification. These individuals are content to do the right things every day even though the results of their doing so are not always visible immediately. These people love, they connect, they take responsibility, they take action, they admit mistakes—and they know that, in time, they should see the fruit of their efforts. These people trust in the principle that "a man reaps what he sows."[2] They don't demand instant results as children do. Instead, being grownups, they stay the course and wait for the harvest. They also remember that a problem may not exist simply to be solved, but it may also exist as a God-given training tool for character growth. Look for the lesson that the problem may be designed to teach you.

---

We sometimes create a problem
where none really exists. So make
sure you have an actual problem.

---

Now that you've acknowledged the value of defining a problem and setting parameters on it, consider these three key questions that will help get you where you want to go.

## DO I ACTUALLY HAVE A PROBLEM?

Does your problem exist in reality or only in your mind? I am not talking here about being psychotic. I am referring to the tendency we sometimes have to create a problem where none really exists. So make sure you have an actual problem. If you don't have a problem, then there is nothing—at least nothing specifically pertaining to your situation—that you need to define or clarify. It's not really helpful to clarify nothing.

Now think back to my original definition of a problem: *a situation in which I want to move from a present state to a desired state, but cannot immediately.* Now consider the following two sorts of situations that appear to be problems, but may not be. Here they are:

**Situations that actually are good and need to be accepted as good**—Sometimes our desire to move from one state to another is misguided, and where we are is actually the better place to be. When that's the case, our desire is the issue to be dealt with, not the situation. Let's say, for example, that you are seventy-five years old and don't have the physical stamina that once enabled you to work seventy hours a week and sleep five hours a night. You want to move from a present state of age-appropriate health to having the constitution of a twenty-five-year-old. So you look for health, nutrition, and exercise regimens in an attempt to regain that energy level. In my mind, the problem is not the lack of energy; the problem is in the desire. Let me explain.

Developmental psychology research suggests that the seventies are a wonderful stage of life that, while characterized by less energy and stamina, instead allows for the enjoyment and embracing of a variety of activities, including reflection on deeper matters, the celebration of cherished relationships, and clear confirmation of one's purpose and mission in life. A person's desire to be twenty-five could therefore be more of an emotional issue rooted either in some kind of resistance to the aging process or in some idealization of how great the twenties were and blindness to the value of anything in later years.

Or suppose you've been dating a guy who wasn't a good match for you, and he breaks up with you. Something inside you may click, and, because you were the one left, not the one leaving, you want to get him back. So you have conversations, arrange meetings, and even try to become who he wants you to be, but he's just not that into you. This probably isn't a problem. It's a reality that frees you up to look elsewhere for a healthier, more satisfying relationship. The emotional problem is more about control than love—control as in *I want to get you back so that I can be the one to break up*. And that never pays off.

So look closely at your current situation. Make sure

that even though the grass appears greener on the other side, it truly is greener and not just spray painted.

**Situations that can't change and must be let go of—** At times, tough circumstances create a loss and there is no turning back: you cannot or, in all likelihood, will not return to the original and desired state. When you are divorced and your ex has remarried, for instance, it is very unlikely that you will eventually marry your first spouse again. There are simply too many realities in the way. Or suppose you are in your forties and have lost a job in a sector overrun by younger people. The odds are very much against your retooling, finding something in that area, and making the money you were used to making. It is probably time to strike out elsewhere, and today many skilled and creative people are successfully doing exactly that.

These scenarios aren't problems. They are situations that need to be let go of, adapted to, and grieved. There is no shame in losing something you cared about. We need to feel sad and shed some tears about something we wanted, longed for, desired, but can't have. Sadness comes when you accept reality rather than insist that reality bow to your interests. The first option is key to mental health;

the second is the path to insanity. Don't go there. Instead, trust me that there comes a point at which all successful problem-solvers stop beating their heads against the giant wall of reality and say, "You win. I will change." These are the people who move on and find fulfillment in other areas of life and in relationships with other people.

## SO WHAT IS THE PROBLEM?

Now let's look at situations where you do want to see changes—and for good reason. Let's look at real problems; it is important to *know what the problem is and clearly define it*. Stating a problem is generally a negative. By negative, I don't mean something you shouldn't do, because some negatives are very good for us (as in, "My lab test came back negative"). I mean that you state the problem in negative language. Here are some examples:

- My marriage is not as close as I wish it were.
- My job is not satisfactory financially or a good match for my talents.
- I don't feel good during the day; I'm always tired and discouraged.

- I don't have enough deep, nurturing relationships.
- My child has behavioral problems that disrupt his life and ours.
- I don't feel close to God even though I know he loves me.

All six of these sentences clearly but succinctly state a problem. Being able to do this is very important and helpful, because then you will have a peg in your mind on which you can hang what you learn in your research and your relationships. In business, the phrase *elevator pitch* means being able to summarize a company's product or service in between floors on an elevator. Like that peg in your mind, an elevator pitch is valuable because it sharpens and maintains focus; it doesn't allow for distractions or rabbit trails.

Recently, I was talking to a friend whose wife left him and filed for divorce. This experience was very painful for him, and it had turned his life upside down. He had, however, done a great job of beginning to pick up the pieces. He was in a healthy small group at his church, he was getting good advice, and he was settling into this new reality. He did, however, ask me for advice about how to deal with his three young kids. He wanted to know how to talk to them about the divorce, answer their questions in developmentally appropriate language, comfort and reassure them, and ascertain if they needed a therapist. Because of our schedules, we set up a thirty-minute phone appointment. I figured that would be more than sufficient, because I knew he had been dealing with good people for a few months, and our conversation would be more focused on the kids than on the entire life issue.

However, when we opened the conversation and I asked him how he was doing, he went into great detail, with great emotion, about what had been happening. But he spoke mostly about the marriage and the relationship with his ex rather than the kids. I felt a great deal of compassion for him, so I did more listening. After all, it was quite apparent that he was not in a place to develop strategies for kid care. Finally, because I had a very tight schedule, I asked him, "How can I help you with the kids?" We went on, and I answered the questions he had. But we didn't spend as much time talking about them as I had wanted to. Even so, were I to do this phone appointment again, I would probably handle the conversation the same way, because I sensed my friend's pain and neediness. Still, the point is that it is always best to, as much as you are able, state your problem in a few words. The clearer you are, the more quickly you will find solutions.

## SERIOUSNESS

Part of defining a problem is determining how serious the situation is. Assessing its importance will prepare you for the solution stages in Step 5; you will better know how much energy and how many resources to apply to the situation.

As I mentioned before, you need to know if this is an urgent crisis that will temporarily take all of your time and attention, or if it is something less urgent and you can have a balanced life while you aggressively pursue a course of action. I use the simple terms *mild, moderate,* and *severe* to make it easier to evaluate the scope and urgency of the situation.

*Mild: The situation bothers me, and it could get worse, so I need to attend to it. But it doesn't disrupt life, work, relationships, and other pursuits. I am just aware of it.* For example, you need to lose ten pounds and get in shape, but you haven't really done anything toward reaching those goals. Or you are dating a woman you really like, but sometimes she seems a little pushy about greater commitment and marriage. A situation labeled "mild" is something to deal with, but it is not yet calling for a big decision.

*Moderate: This situation comes up a lot and gets in the way of life as I want to live it. It isn't a crisis, but I find that it slows down my personal growth and my progress toward my goals.* An example is your marriage that has lots of good aspects.

---

None of us keeps the needle
on perfect reality all the time. So
ask a few mature people to help
you understand how bad
the problem is—and isn't.

---

Perhaps you parent together well and get along OK, but there is little passion or excitement about each other. The relationship feels especially empty when there is no person, activity, or noise to distract you from the disconnect. Or you know that your company may be downsizing. Although the boss tells you you're valuable, you wonder if you should be taking action just in case the downsize means no more work for you.

*Severe: The situation is a crisis requiring enormous amounts of my time, energy, and focus. This crisis could potentially overtake my life. In fact, this situation could even get worse before it gets better.* An example would be a major health issue, an out-of-control child experimenting with drugs, or having the family's breadwinner laid off with no job prospects on the horizon.

None of us keeps the needle on perfect reality all the time. You may be an eternal optimist who minimizes things, or you may struggle with anxiety and tend to make matters far worse in your mind, an option we'll deal with in Step 4. So ask a few mature people to help you make sure you understand how bad the problem is—and isn't. You may need then to either get moving more quickly... or slow down and trust God, his process of change, and his timing.

# WHAT DO I WANT?

In response to this more positive question about your problem, you describe the desired state, what you want the situation to be like. Desire is a great thing and, I believe, a gift from God. In fact, I hope you have desires that aren't rooted in solving a problem; I hope you have desires that are just good desires: *I want to create a sustainable and solid business; I want to write a book; I want to contribute my time to helping the poor;* or *I want some great vacation experiences.*

Asking yourself the "What do I want?" question helps you clarify your thoughts in a different way than the "What is the problem?" question does. The desire-based question sensitizes you to your motivations, your energy, and your longings. It hooks you into the internal drive that will propel you toward action and results. No desire, no solution-oriented behaviors. Lots of desire, lots of solution-oriented behaviors.

Let's marry the responses to these two questions for a fuller look at defining where you are and where you want to be:

- My marriage is not as close as it needs to be. *I want an intimate marriage with my spouse.*
- My job is not satisfactory financially or a good match for my talents. *I want a job that pays well and fits who I am.*
- I don't feel good during the day; I'm always tired and discouraged. *I want to feel energetic and OK throughout my day.*
- I don't have enough deep, nurturing relationships. *I want a few relationships that are safe and growth-producing for me.*
- My child has behavioral problems that disrupt his life and ours. *I want my child to be happy and able to exercise self-control over his behavior.*
- I don't feel close to God, even though I know he loves me. *I want to experience God's love for me.*

Do you see the benefit of asking both types of questions? You state the problem, and then you state what you want. Wanting a good solution is not a sign of selfishness. You simply want bad things to improve, and there is no harm in that. Remember: *if you only think about the problem and never about your desires, you are constantly playing defense in life, not offense.* Life isn't fundamentally about solving problems. Life is about God, relationships, and purpose. Solving problems gets the speed bumps out of the way so that you can live the life God wants for you.

So keep these questions in mind: Do I have a problem? What is it? What do I want? Keep your answers simple, keep them focused, build a strong fence, and you'll find yourself well on the way to a solution to your problem.

# Break Free from Fear

*The only thing we have to fear is fear itself—*
*nameless, unreasoning, unjustified terror*
*which paralyzes needed efforts to*
*convert retreat into advance.*
—*Franklin D. Roosevelt*

A friend of mine was starting a new business and asked me to help her. She was moving from an extensive background and experience base in education to a coaching career. She had retooled well and, on a training level, was ready to go. We talked about her business plan and her marketing. She wanted to create a website as part of that marketing effort. The project went pretty well for a few weeks. She is a competent person who worked hard to get things off the ground. Except for the website. It had stalled early in the game. Whenever we talked about the project, she was excited and showed me lots of progress in the financials, in defining the services she would offer, and in the contacts she was making. But, at the end of our talk, the website would get just a few seconds of airtime, and she would say, "I'm getting to it. Let's talk about that later." Or something to that effect.

Finally, I became a little concerned. The business was moving forward on several fronts, but soon the lack of a compelling website could significantly handicap her progress. So we had a conversation focused specifically on the site development. I asked her why it seemed so far behind. Not sure at first, she thought it might be because she was not yet very Web savvy, though she said she would catch up. But that didn't really make sense, because she hadn't caught up for a while. We probed deeper into the problem. Finally, she blurted out, "You know, I'm avoiding the site. I am really afraid of this."

"Why?" I asked.

"Because I don't know what I'm doing. I know how to coach, and how to get organized, and how to speak to groups. But I don't know anything about developing a website."

Pressing her a little, I said, "Maybe not, but lots of people either go to a simple Web design site and use a template, or they hire a designer and tell that person what they want. There are lots of simple and inexpensive options these days. That can't be it." I was trying to get her beyond the reasons—past her head to her heart —because I suspected that something emotional was going on.

Finally, she began to tear up a little and said, "I am afraid I'll be a dummy."

"A dummy?" I asked. "You have a master's degree and you're really smart. Where does that message come from?"

She thought for a moment and said, "I've always been comfortable doing what I do well in areas I know well. But when I try something I have no experience in, I tell myself that I'm an idiot—and that everyone else thinks so as well."

Then she told me about growing up with parents who expected excellence in everything she did. They were extremely bright and somewhat rigid people. There was no room in their minds for a learning curve. *Get it right the first or second time, or you're a dummy* was the unspoken creed. This sort of family culture creates a perfectionist who becomes paralyzed with fear when she encounters a new situation.

The insights my friend gained while talking about her childhood made all the difference in the world for her. Yes, she had a problem: she was not moving ahead on her website project. But the basis of the problem wasn't a lack of experience with Web development or her inability to define the business. She was simply stuck in fear and couldn't get out. Once the fear and its roots were

---

You must break free from your fear
in order to solve your problem.

---

unearthed, we were able to spend some time resolving her fear using the principles in this chapter, and she moved ahead on the website.

Here is the point: *You must break free from your fear in order to solve your problem.* It is very common that some sort of fear or anxiety is the reason why people have a relational, career, or family issue that they can't seem to work out or work through. In fact, my experience has shown that fear slows down problem solving far more than any other emotion does, which is why fear has its own chapter in this book.

By the way, of course not all fear and anxiety are bad. If you are an impulsive person, you may need a little anxiety to rein things in. Also, since I am the father of two teenage boys, one of my goals is to actually create fear in them, because they often don't worry enough about future consequences! The reality-based fear that makes you think ahead about your actions and your life is a good thing. Knowing we have to pay the rent or the mortgage on the first of the month keeps us actively working or seeking work. That knowledge gives us focus and energy. It's fear that is not tethered to reality that is the problem.

Also by the way, I will be using the words "fear" and "anxiety" interchangeably in this overview. On a technical level, some experts say that fear has a specific object (someone points a gun at you) and anxiety does not (it's a general feeling that things are unsafe). But I have talked to too many people who are very anxious about a specific financial upset or broken relationship for that definition to be accurate. I think the difference between fear and anxiety is more a matter of focus. Fear is directed toward the situation ("I am scared of the economic downturn.

---

Obsessive thoughts about what
could go wrong can keep you
thinking rather than acting.

---

We don't know how bad it will get or when it will turn around"), and feelings of anxiety focus on your own experience ("I am anxious about the downturn, so anxious that I don't sleep well, I feel agitated, and I can't focus at work").

Now, back to the matter at hand, here are some of the reasons why fear is a solution-killer:

- *Fear paralyzes you.* Fear keeps you from being decisive, and obsessive thoughts about what could go wrong can keep you thinking rather than acting.
- *Fear clouds your judgment.* Fear can make you worry

about the wrong things, and it can make you give too much weight to something that isn't that important. Still hearing their voices from the past, my friend was too worried about what her parents might think to move ahead with a website that would help her fulfill her goals.

- *Fear makes you go for the short term instead of the long term.* Have you ever committed to the wrong person in love or in business because that person was available, you were anxious, and you couldn't wait for the right situation?

- *Fear limits your creativity.* Figuratively speaking, if there is anything you need in order to fix your cell phone, it is creativity—a new way of looking at things from a fresh and different perspective. When you can't get fear out of your mind, though, you think only in terms of safety, survival, and security. You don't think, "What's a different and sort of crazy way to look at my situation?" You think instead, "How can I protect myself?"

One more thing. There is a reason why we address fear at this point in the problem-solving sequence, why it comes after the chapter on setting parameters on the problem and before the chapter on creating a solution. This is the spot because I have seen that *when we face the true realities of our problem, we naturally and immediately experience anxiety and fear.* That is, when you see the details about what you don't have or don't like in your life, how serious the circumstances might be, and how much you desire things to be different, your life situation can be daunting and scary. Imagine going to the doctor, getting tested, and receiving results that you didn't want to hear. You have more information than you had before, and you feel overwhelmed. Likewise, now that you know more about the problem you want to solve and are probably feeling overwhelmed, it's time to deal with the fear that besets everyone at this juncture. Let's understand a little more about what fear is so we can combat it successfully.

## THE DNA OF FEAR

Fear is basically a danger signal. It alerts you to something that could harm you, and it makes you more vigilant, more clearheaded. Fear also triggers an increase in your adrenaline in case you need more quick energy. And fear heightens the sense that something may be about to happen that you can't control, so you must be ready. Think about a group of zebras catching the scent of a lion. They can't control the lion, but they can control where they will be, and they run away. But we human beings can't tolerate being too afraid for too long a period of time. The adrenaline just doesn't work after a while, we lose energy, we stop being as sharply focused, and sometimes we simply give up. You can't run the mental engine at 8000 rpm all the time. There will be some sort of breakdown.

So fear can be your friend, but the wrong kinds and the wrong amount of fear will keep you from solving problems the right way. For example, if you are overwhelmed and panicky about your job, the future, a relationship, or your health, you will not think clearly. Instead, you'll simply go into the "fight or flight" mode, which means you will either do something irrational and rash, or you'll avoid the problem and risk having it get worse.

For other people, fear gets tangled with their own perfectionism. When these folks encounter a problem, they worry more about making a mistake and causing the situation to get worse than about coming up with a solid solution. So these people don't do anything because they can't figure out how to solve the problem perfectly. I worked with a couple whose young daughter had huge temper tantrums whenever she wouldn't get her way. Her parents had a perfectionistic bent, though, and didn't want to do anything that would damage her self-image. They didn't realize that a healthy self-image comes from being loved and learning self-control, not from being allowed to be out of control. This mom and dad worried

_____

We human beings
can't tolerate being too afraid
for too long a period.

_____

constantly about "the best way to talk to Steffy." Finally, I said, "Time's up. You've thought of a lot of ways to deal with her, and I think the plan you have now [it involved a conversation about love, support, realistic expectations, clear boundaries, and appropriate consequences] is good enough. Have the talk and implement the plan. It's not perfect, but she will get worse by the time you have a perfect plan." They talked with Steffy that week. The course of action they had planned was tough, as you can imagine, but they got through it. And I honestly don't know how long they would have procrastinated about solving their problem had their perfectionism and fear won out.

## TOOLS FOR BANISHING FEAR

Let's look at four tools I believe go a long way to help when your fears threaten to keep you from aggressively and creatively moving ahead to solve your problem.

**1. Trust in God.** God is larger than any problem we have. He has larger shoulders for your problem than you do: "Cast all your anxiety on him because he cares for you."[1] I love the word "cast" in that verse: in the Greek, it refers to the very physical action of throwing or hurling. The idea is to forcefully reject playing God here and to instead throw your problem to him: "God, I just can't do this myself. The problem is beyond me, and I can't bear it, so I give it up to you. Here it comes." And he will catch it and carry it. Trusting God always reduces fear.

**2. Unload on a few safe people.** When you are feeling anxious, the worst thing you can do is be alone with your anxiety. Your thoughts easily escalate into the worst-possible scenarios. A business friend of mine would not tell his friends this, but he did tell me: "First, I have a problem. Then my anxiety kicks in, and I keep it to

---

Fear contained by others is
always reduced. Fear borne alone
will grow.

---

myself, and it is soon a crisis. Then, when the anxiety is in full swing, I am still by myself, and I imagine that my family and I will soon be living in a motel room, eating from a hot plate."

While some people do experience that unfortunate turn of events and need our compassion and help, most people won't. In reality, this friend was a professional man of good character who was very competent and intelligent. As of this writing, he has had to tighten up matters, but he is nowhere near where his anxiety told him he would be. Furthermore, I have worked with him and encouraged him to tell others how he is feeling before his anxiety becomes too intense.

This practice of unloading on a few safe people is simply a matter of being heard and understood. In psychology, it is called *containing*, a word that simply means having a few good people listen to your fear and anxiety, in an unvarnished state without any editing or concern for political correctness. These people "contain" your anxieties, and their presence with you lets you know that you are not alone. Have you ever unloaded your concerns in a weak moment to someone who had the ability to listen well, with no advice, and yet you felt better? That person contained you, and fear contained by others is always reduced. Fear borne alone will grow. Utilize those right people we talked about at Step 2. They will be glad to listen and contain.

**3. Add structure.** You might be surprised, but a predictable schedule and a regular rhythm for your days—including work, exercise, fun activities, and meals with friends—can do much to reduce anxiety. Structure greatly reduces anxiety because anxiety is rooted in the feeling that we have lost control. Anxiety grows when we feel we are helpless and have no choices. In severe cases, people who don't feel they have any choices at all go into a very disruptive panic mode. When, however, you add structure, you give life a normalcy, and you gain a handle on the choices and control you do have. When you know you will go to work, attend certain meetings, and make certain calls at specific times, your sense that you are not helpless grows. And in your particular problem situation, the plan that you develop to resolve that problem will also decrease your anxiety.

As I mentioned earlier, fear reduces us to thinking impulsively and superficially. For example, I worked with a professional woman who reported to a pretty toxic vice president. He was controlling and critical. Afraid of his anger and put-downs, she simply avoided him in order to survive. Even without a parachute, though, she was ready to leave the company because interacting with him was so uncomfortable. I told her, "The reality is that this is a good job for you even with this person in the company. Let's work on adding some structures to what you are already doing; let's see if you can improve the workplace for yourself instead of leaving because you are afraid of this man." She and I figured out what her fears of confrontation were about in the first place, we went through a series of trainings to prepare her to confront a superior, we learned the company's due diligence process if he did not respond, she found out how to leave a paper trail if she had to go to his superior, and so forth. As she took these steps, her anxiety decreased: the structure gave her a sense of control.

———

Solving your problem will undoubtedly require you to change your schedule and the ways you invest your time. But when you adapt, you conserve energy.

———

**4. Adapt to reality.** Solving your problem will undoubtedly require you to change your schedule and the ways you invest your time. This process—called adaptation—means not fighting the changes but, even if doing so is uncomfortable, adjusting to it. When you adapt, you conserve energy. Think of reality being a river and you are a canoe: don't paddle upstream, but figure out a way to navigate that doesn't fight the river's current, but instead uses its power.

Case in point. Having kids who will be entering the workforce soon, I have always hated it when reporters say, "It looks bleak for the next generation. They won't be as successful as their parents." Young people just don't need to be discouraged from ambition and achievement during this developmental stage of life. So, whenever the topic has come up, I told them, "You know what this means for you? It means less competition at the top. Go for it!" Now when they consider their economic future, hopefully this perspective on adaptation will help my sons stay motivated rather than tempting them to settle for the status quo.

To close, I want to challenge you to be intentional about defeating your fear. Realize it is in all of us. Only people who are in denial, or who are really foolish, don't experience anxiety. So be aware of your fear and resolve it. This will free you up to take the next step toward solving your problem.

STEP 5:

# Control What You Own

*Action springs not from thought, but from a
readiness for responsibility.*
*—Dietrich Bonhoeffer*

I was helping a woman whose marriage was failing. They
weren't ready to file, but the situation was serious. She and
her husband were at odds over some basic personality differences, and the antagonism was escalating. She saw him
as very inattentive and detached; he experienced her as
nagging and critical. She was more interested than he in
working with someone to improve the relationship; he
just wanted to disconnect and avoid the issues. Though
it's always best to work with both spouses, we worked
with what we had, which was the wife alone. The problem
was, I couldn't get her to focus on the things she could

control to help the relationship. She was so upset and hurt by his actions that he was all she could talk about.

"So let's talk about your alternatives."

"How can I get him stop his silent treatment and his being gone so much?"

"Well, I want us to go over what options you have."

"What will it take to make him get his act together?"

"I know this is a really difficult situation. Let's look at your choices."

"What can I say to make him love me and want to work this out?"

I knew I needed to take a different tack. I said, "What we are doing is not helping you. Either we need to dedicate some time for you to process your pain and hurt and get to solutions later, or we can figure out a way for that part to go to your support group, so you can get their love and care. Or we can just try harder to focus on solutions now. I totally understand if you need to get the pain out, because your life has been turned upside down. But I wanted to help you do some problem solving today, and I don't want to lead you to think that we'll have any plan by the time this meeting ends. You tell me what is best for you."

She was quiet a minute, and then she said, "This is what always happens . . ."

"What's that?"

"I never get past this point with anyone I talk to. I just go over and over what he's been doing and how I want to change him. I need to move past this."

She was right, and it was a valuable insight for her. As we talked, she realized that she was trying to control something she had no control over. That something was her husband's behavior, including his decisions and his attitudes. But none of us can control another person's behavior. We can try to influence people we care about. We can talk to them. We can be vulnerable with them. And we can set limits and boundaries with them, so that they are forced to face the realities of their actions. But, ultimately, *we waste precious problem-solving resources when we try to change or control another person.*

This insight changed the direction of my friend's problem-solving mission. She let go of what she had no power or right to control, and she focused on what she could control. She took charge of what was hers, what she "owned," so to speak. She took control over what was inside her skin, which is basically all any of us have control over. This change of focus was not quick or easy for her, but she persevered. She worked hard on what she could control, and eventually he came to the counseling sessions with her. In time, they began to reconnect again, and I don't think that would ever have happened if she had not started focusing on what she could control.

This principle doesn't apply only to marriage; it applies to any problem in life. You can't control the economic downturn, crazy people, the existence of death, the marketplace, or the weather. Yet you have to solve problems in life even though there are chess pieces on the board that aren't yours to move. So let's look at what you do possess and can control. You will be pleasantly surprised by all the progress you can make *even when you aren't in charge of all the moving pieces.*

I always like to remind myself that my kids, on the verge of manhood, have made it this far reasonably intact. They are good people: I like who they are deciding to be, and I look forward to being less of an authority and more of a friend to them as they become more autonomous. My wife and I have been involved parents, and we did what most parents do to keep the ship afloat. Yet I am always amazed by how much we didn't control during all those years they were growing up: all the times they were away from us, making their own choices; the medical and health issues we had no control over; the influence of culture on them; what their friends told them when we weren't around; and, ultimately, their own thoughts, values, and actions. It's scary to think about all we didn't and don't control, but it would have driven us crazy to try to control what wasn't ours in the first place.

So let's look at what each one of us does own.

## WHAT IS YOURS

Since the purpose of this book is solving problems, I want to focus on those things that are yours to control and use that will help you do just that. Here are those things that belong to you, things that you truly own and can control.

**Your heart**—This is the deepest part of you, of any of us. It is the essence of who you are. It encompasses your inner life, your thoughts, your secrets, and your feelings. No one except you can own your heart, so "above all else, guard your heart, for it is the wellspring of life."[1] Why does this matter? It matters because I find that so many people bypass their hearts when they encounter a problem. They worry about, and try to control, anything and everything except what is inside them. In so doing, they disown themselves and, ultimately, their hearts. You can solve a problem without addressing your heart, but you risk solving the wrong problem.

Consider the experience of a man whose story included a cocaine addiction. As is often the case, he was in denial; he didn't consider cocaine a problem. Since he didn't see it as a problem, nothing changed. His wife, however, considered it a major problem. She hated him being on drugs, and she hated what it was doing to their life together. But she didn't have the addiction herself, so she couldn't send herself to rehab. What she could and did do was tell him, "I love you with all my heart, but I am terrified by your drug use. It is shattering me and our relationship. I feel alone and all by myself in this marriage, and I miss how we used to be. If you choose to go to rehab, I will support you. But until then, though I love you, I will not live with you, and I need you to move out and have no contact with me until you get help."

Do you see how she was in touch with her heart? She was vulnerable and caring as she spoke with her husband

and told him that she would not stand for his drug use. She was a picture of grace and truth, all from her heart. The man told me he knew she meant it, so he skipped the moving out part and got help immediately.

---

You can solve a problem without addressing your heart, but you risk solving the wrong problem.

---

The point is, when you're solving a problem, start with your heart. It can be wrong, but better being wrong than ignoring who you are as you attempt to solve your problem.

**Your values**—The foundational truths on which you base your life are your values. These ultimate realities serve as an anchor for your decisions and problem-solving behaviors. So think through and know what your values are. Here are some examples:

· God and his ways give purpose to my life and guide my paths.

- Relationships are primary to the kind of life I want to live.
- Honesty and holiness are nonnegotiable.
- I allow others freedom to make their own life, career, and relational choices, and I want that freedom for myself as well.
- I have a God-given mission in life, and by his grace I will accomplish it.
- Mistakes and failure are to be expected, and forgiveness of others and of myself will be my response.

In my coaching and consulting work, I have seen that a problem is sometimes solved simply by filtering it through the company's values, so to speak. There are decisions you know from the get-go that you will and won't make, because your values have made those decisions for you. For example, I know a man whose fiancée was flirting. When he was with her, she would say inappropriate things to other men and tell him she didn't see anything wrong with it. Her behavior hurt his feelings and bothered him. He found himself wondering if he could trust her. When we discussed it, he said, "I know what I'll do. I'll start flirting, too, and show her how it feels." While I understood the idea, I had to say, "Think about this. You value faithfulness and security in your life, relationships, and career. I don't think you want to go with that solution." He thought about it and said, "What was I thinking? I'd better find another way." Just being reminded of his values helped clarify what he wanted to do—and didn't want to do—to solve his problem.

**Your choices**—Ultimately, your choices and decisions are your property. You can't make someone who is "just not into you" fall in love with you. You can't force the

---

You can only choose for you,
and one kind of choice is how you
will respond to whatever you didn't
get to choose!

---

company to reconsider your layoff. You can't make the bank reconsider the loan application. You can't choose for your kids that they pick up after themselves. You can only choose for you, and one kind of choice is how you will respond to whatever you didn't get to choose! In a way, this truth may be discouraging. We often think, *Why don't our problem people just see the situation correctly and get it together? Don't they recognize that they are making bad decisions?* And then we strategize ways to help them see that our opinion for them is the right way. Most of this activity is doomed to failure, because our so-called problem people experience our encouragement as nagging rather than good advice, or as manipulation rather than a helpful, caring strategy. These folks invariably dig in their heels—just as you and I probably would. None of us responds well to someone who comes across as a parent figure, thwarting our own choices and freedoms.

So remember this when you are facing your problem: if you are spending more energy on what your problem person is doing (as my friend in the bad marriage was), you are out of balance. The bulk of your energy needs to be focused on you—on how you may be contributing to the problem or the problem person's behavior; how you can have a good life with a person who isn't healthy; how you can respond to that person's words, actions, and attitudes in the best ways possible; and how you can keep their problem from holding your happiness hostage.

Given that, then, a good way to own your choices and to only choose for yourself is to never waste your energy on trying to control or choose for someone else. Instead, focus on your choices and your decisions. Doing so can be a significantly effective move toward solving the problems you need to solve. Instead of feeling impotent and helpless to make someone "get it" (and the reality is that you are impotent and helpless to make that happen), you can feel a sense of control and even accomplishment from the right choices you make for yourself.

Now let's look at the situations above and provide a "your choice" perspective for them:

- *He's just not that into me, and I need to change that.* I will accept his lack of feelings for me and move on to where there are guys who will be into me.
- *The company needs to reconsider my layoff.* I made my best case for keeping my position, and I will be aggressive in looking for a job elsewhere. I will not burn bridges with my former employer and may even ask for their help and a recommendation.
- *The bank doesn't understand that I qualify for the loan.* Whatever I think about my financial state, I need

to accept that this bank sees it differently. So I'll go to other lenders or find other sources of money.

- *My kids need to be considerate and pick up after themselves.* While I can't make my kids do this, I do have leverage here! I can choose to withhold privileges until those chores are done.

In each case, notice that when you focus on your choices, you have to let something go. That something is the wish to fix, control, rescue, enable, or choose for someone else. Letting that go is not necessarily easy or fun, but doing so will free up your energy and focus, diverting you away from something you can't control and directing you to your own life, which you can. Let go of trying to control and make choices for others. Instead, choose to only choose for yourself.

**Your time**—Time may be one of the most finite resources we have. I don't want to be negative, but we're all going to die before we reach 130 or so. You can add friends all your life, you have so many choices ahead of you, and your fortunes may rise and fall, but time can't be changed. I'd love to add a few hundred years to my time allotment, because then I could spread out some of my long-term projects. But adding those extra couple centuries just won't happen. We may as well accept it and not worry about it, since, as Jesus said, "Who of you by worrying can add a single hour to his life?"[2] So be conscious that time is precious and careful about how much time you take to solve your problem.

We all have the tendency to make two mistakes with time. First, we fall into the trap of thinking there is more time than we need ahead of us. When there is a problem to address that involves blood, sweat, tears, and real effort, we often think, "I'll get to it just as soon as I organize the files on the hard drive. Then I'll be more ready for action." That overly optimistic view is rooted in avoidance. Realize that you have limited time on this earth and therefore a limited window for addressing your problem, and you don't want that window to close before you solve your problem.

The second mistake we make is thinking, "I don't have enough time! There are too many demands on me." This is a common concern for any breathing human being, and there may actually be too many demands on you. But do this: grab your calendar and, with someone who loves you and will be honest, review the past couple weeks calendar. It can be a real "aha" moment when you find some hours that either weren't organized well or, more likely, were sacrificed on the altar of keeping someone else happy—someone who could have made it just fine without you. Fix these two mistakes, and you will be more in control of your time.

We human beings are all control freaks by nature, and that's been the case from the beginning. We see the desire to be in charge and make our own decisions back in the garden when God wanted to show Adam and Eve which tree they should eat from. But the more you give up what isn't yours, the more freely you can move toward what truly is yours.

# Create a Pass/Fail Plan

*There is no such thing as luck.*
*There is only adequate or inadequate preparation*
*to cope with a statistical universe.*
*—Robert Heinlein*

There are those individuals who, when faced with a life problem, do a good job of researching, thinking creatively, and kicking ideas around with friends. Simply going through that process will produce solutions for them at some rate of success. Then there are those people who, in addition to doing those three things, create a plan. In my experience, the second group will have a considerably higher success rate when it comes to solving their problems. A specific plan will take you farther down the road to a solution.

If you are like me, this might be the chapter you are likely to skip over. You have probably read many articles or books on how to make a workable plan to help you set and reach your goals.[1] You may be familiar with all the helpful products and software programs that successfully take you through a plan for getting where you want to get in life. You may even have professional experience in drawing up business plans or financial plans. None of that matters, because this chapter doesn't rehash all that. Instead, here you will find a framework not only for dealing with the psychological realities of making a plan but also for actually making an effective and beneficial problem-solving plan for yourself.

## PASS/FAIL

Basically, you need to create a plan and write it out because that is the best way to keep focused on the specific steps that will help you solve your problem. I call this the *pass/fail* method. When you know what action steps to take, when you have memorized them in a Word document, spreadsheet, or notebook, and when you know you must take those steps at a certain time, you have put yourself on this pass/fail system. Simply put, you either take a step by a certain date, or you don't. You pass if you do the action, and you fail if you don't. Taking this cut-and-dried approach is not being anal retentive or rigid. It is not being shaming or condemning or legalistic. This pass/fail method is a means of aligning yourself with reality. It is drawing a line in the sand so that you can monitor your progress, be accountable, and have the security of knowing you are walking through the steps of a workable plan. Creative types like artists, musicians, and writers all have deadlines of some sort, and many set incremental deadlines for themselves so they can do their craft in bite-sized increments. Pass/fail is your friend and theirs. Without it, you will never know how far along you are or if you are still on course. Actually, I call the lack of a plan fail/fail, because it almost never works.

## THE ELEMENTS

Most problem-solving plans have five universal elements that fit any situation. I list them below, and to flesh them out, I will take you through one man's experience of a common problem.

Gene, a software expert in his thirties, has been laid off. He and his wife, Donna, have two young children and a mortgage. Donna works part-time as a teacher. The couple has Gene's severance package and enough liquidity to last them six months. They have some long-term investments that they don't want to touch if they don't have to. So, with a runway of half a year, they qualify: they definitely have a problem.

Let's assume that Gene and Donna have been through the rest of the book's steps: they're paying attention to their feelings, they are connected to some good folks, they know the nature of the problem, they are done with fear, and they understand what they are in control of and what they're not. Now they're ready for Step 6.

**Set the goal.** Step 3 addresses stating what the problem is and stating what you want. Remember that your problem is something that is an obstacle for you, something that gets in the way of your ability to satisfy a desire that matters to you. Looking back at the desire as you expressed it in Step 3, state your goal in a way that it is both meaningful and measurable.

For Gene and Donna, a reasonable goal would be *Within six months, we want to be generating $X,XXX income* *a month for our short-term and our long-term needs.* That is simple, clear, and pass/fail in nature. It is a goal they can shoot for and see if they are making progress. This sounds like a statement of the obvious, because it is—but don't miss this point. It takes effort to state a measurable goal, establish a time frame, and set a deadline, and sometimes we just don't get around to doing it. Think about a

---

It takes effort to state a measurable goal, establish a time frame, and set a deadline.

---

failed attempt to regularly work out at the gym. Compare that experience to the time you actually wrote out "Three months from now, I want to be XXX pounds and able to do cardio for forty-five minutes without collapsing." The road to failure is paved with good intentions.

**Creatively consider the options.** This is the brainstorming element of developing your plan. All ideas are welcome, and the more creative, the better.

I often use a flip chart with people so they can see the blank space and then fill it up with their ideas. The less clutter on the page when you start, the more solutions you will find—and be sure to restrain yourself on two counts at this phase. First, don't think about how realistic the idea is yet. The internal CPA we all have must wait his turn in line until this options phase is over. Otherwise, creativity can be dampened and even discouraged. Second, don't ask yourself, "What are other people in my position doing?" Do that later, but not now. Why? Because doing what other people are doing feeds into our desire for a quick answer so we can be done with it.

Unless you are in your car stalled on a railroad track and the train is bearing down on you, take some time to look at your problem as an opportunity to actually *end up better off than you were before*. Don't shy away from that thought. It happens all the time. I know many people who handled their problem in such a way that their situation was much improved over where they were before the issue arose. So instead of being practical, go with "What is a way to get the income that we haven't considered?"

At this point, Gene and Donna consider lots of options. They call their friends, get ideas, and collect suggestions. No idea is too unrealistic. In the end, their top ones are:

- An aggressive job search in the same field with other companies
- A short-term job that will provide income while Gene is looking
- Retraining for a different career path
- Creating a small business (some kind of boutique) that they can own together
- Donna moving from part-time to full-time work
- Selling the house and downsizing to live more modestly
- Relocating to a less expensive part of the country

**Make a decision.** This step is not guaranteed to happen automatically; you must be intentional about setting yourself a deadline for landing on a decision. If you don't, you run several risks:

- The risk of *infinite research*, that is, constantly looking for the next idea that will work, a search that could go on forever

- The risk of *idealism*, which has to do with the fear of making the wrong move and not finding the "right" answer

- The risk of *anesthetizing the situation* by brainstorming. Here, a person feels so relieved that he has done something and written down ideas, that he loses the healthy anxiety he needs in order to forge ahead, and the process stalls out. It's a little like, "I started working out today after two years of inactivity, so I'll reward myself with a milkshake."

Even if you're not 100 percent sure that your plan will work, make your best, educated, and prayed-over decision. Besides, a 100-percent-sure plan doesn't exist anyway, so go for something that stands up to good thought and careful deliberation.

Let's say that Gene and Donna opt for the first alternative on their list and choose to put their resources into helping Gene stay in the same sector. Software is not going away, Gene is very competent, and he likes the work. So now they have committed to a plan, and it comes with the risk of not finding what they want. But it is not an impulsive risk; it is a measured one.

**Create a strategy.** We create a strategy simply by setting forth the steps we need to take to get where we want to go. Pass/fail in nature, the strategy breaks the goal down into smaller pieces that make it easier for you to keep a life, yet know that you are constantly moving toward the solution to your problem.

This step of creating a strategy, though, is where lots of people have trouble developing a workable plan. If you are a visionary type, a right-brainer, a person who loves to be in the moment and is not bothered by details, or if you feel constrained by daily or weekly tasks, you need to bear down some here. This element is really not optional if you're serious about solving a problem, whether it's a family, financial, emotional, or relational issue. But if you are by nature a strategic planner, you know what to do, and you probably won't have any trouble at all.

When you start working on your strategy—and there are many approaches—the basics are to allocate your resources (how much time, attention, and money can you dedicate to the strategy?) and outline actions that will lead to success. Most people need to take at least one action per week, and probably several, to experience meaningful progress.

When dealing with personal and relational problems, some people resist strategic thinking. It seems impersonal: *how can I strategize love?* You are right: you can't. But you can strategize actions that bear the fruit of love. That is why couples plan date nights and don't merely wait until the time seems good. It is why people who want to be closer to God go to church, find a time during the day to pray, and don't wait to worship until they're in the mood. These actions that you plan don't rule your life or make you a robot. You will still have lots of room to be spontaneous, emotional, and alive in the moment. But if you have a problem, you won't solve it with spontaneity and emotion. Schedule the time to work on resolving the issue.

The other problem to be aware of is *disillusionment,* a kind of "Is that all there is?" feeling of discouragement. This disillusionment comes from that part of all of us that engages in magical thinking. It begins when we are children, and it is evident in our love of miracles and jaw-dropping experiences that encourage our hearts and reaffirm our faith in God and people. We want: a check to arrive in the mail . . . a person we are alienated from to say he misses us and wants to reconnect . . . a job opening to come out of the blue. These things do happen from time to time, but they are not the norm. Consider, though, the sort of magic that is abundant in God's world today: the birth of a child; a profound and deeply moving time with the Lord; a friend who calls to say, "I'm thinking of you"; a marriage proposal; a medical miracle. Stories—true stories like these—help keep us going in life.

*If you have a problem, you won't solve it with spontaneity and emotion. Schedule the time to work on resolving the issue.*

And we certainly don't think about strategy the way we think of God's kind of magic. *I had a magical, miraculous strategic meeting at work* sounds like an oxymoron. But strategy truly is miraculous, and it must be appreciated and embraced as the gift and tool it is. I always go to Jesus' parable of the growing seed for a picture of one of God's miraculous strategies:

This is what the kingdom of God is like. A man scatters seed on the ground. Night and day, whether he sleeps or gets up, the seed sprouts and grows, though he does not know how. All by itself the soil produces grain—first the stalk, then the head, then the full kernel in the head. As soon as the grain is ripe, he puts the sickle to it, because the harvest has come.[2]

The idea of this parable is that *change happens over time and is often unseen.* When God wants a good thing to happen to us, we do our own part: we make our plan, we face hard things, and we take our steps. Then he does his work and, though we don't know every molecular step involved, the harvest comes. Look at strategy that way. Little by little, step by step, your weekly, daily, or hourly diligence in doing the right things will result in a miracle.

Now back to Gene and Donna. In their situation, Gene dedicates his full-time energies to the search for a job. He develops a multimodal plan involving face-to-face meetings, phone calls to various friends and colleagues, working with an executive search firm, searching through the online job sites, and accessing professional social media. Gene knows how many contacts he wants to make every day. He knows when he will have his resume completed and ready to send out. He knows that in thirty days, he should be contacting his key contacts a second time. The strategy Gene and Donna created is not just a course of actions; it is a course of the right actions. Yours must be too.

STEP 7:

# Do the Right Things

*Never confuse movement with action.*
*—Ernest Hemingway*

I recently encountered a problem with Casey, one of our two Labrador retrievers. She wasn't coming to her meals. That was very unusual, Labs being food addicts by nature. Whenever I called them to eat, Heidi would race to the food bowl, but Casey was nowhere to be found. Finally, I would locate her, coax her into coming to dinner, and then everything would be fine. I didn't know what was wrong. *Was she tired of the same old food regimen? Was she not interested in eating?* I couldn't figure it out.

The answer came when I walked into the living room where Casey was sleeping on the floor. I called her and she didn't stir. In fact, Heidi, who was in another room, heard and came up to me. So I called Casey in a significantly louder voice, and she hopped up and came to me. Casey is losing her hearing, sad to say. So, in our family, we are all adjusting to that. We talk a little louder to her, and we get in front of her so we will be in her line of sight when we want to play with her or take her for a walk. Casey's appetite is fine. She wants to eat. Her problem has nothing to do with motivation or the menu, but something else.

Casey was designed to go for her food, to act and "do" to get it. She doesn't need a lesson in the importance of a good diet. She experiences hunger, and it is a straight line to solving her hunger problem. She takes action on her "feed me" plan—unless there is an obstacle, such as a hearing problem, in the way. Humans are designed according to the same principle: action follows some motivator, whether it is a need, a passion, a desire, a pain, or a problem. When we have a reason to, we are to "do" whatever is needed. When God created Adam and Eve, he said, "Be fruitful and increase in number; fill the earth and subdue it."[1] This is, as an engineer would say, a design feature. We are born to do, born to act. Getting out of bed in the morning to go to work is often a pain, but we do it because it brings things we need. We are not just relaters to people; we are doers in life.

That's why this chapter focuses on doing your plan, on taking action, because that is absolutely necessary to conquering our problems. Lots of literature on taking action basically says, "If you aren't taking the right steps, you must not want to, or you are lazy, or you aren't trying hard enough. So get off your butt and work your plan."

---

> Taking action is absolutely
> necessary to conquering
> our problems.

---

That is the sum and substance of a message designed to help people get moving, and, as a business coach, I know that sometimes not trying hard truly is the issue that needs to be addressed. Certainly each of us can be lazy. But most of the time I have seen that "not trying" is a minor issue, not a major one. If you are dealing with hard-core juvenile delinquents who have entitlement issues, reject all authority, and have no work ethic, a greater percentage may not be trying. But most people struggling with the problems we are addressing in this book are trying hard, and they do want to change.

So here is a guideline to help you take action: *Pay as much attention to removing your obstacles as you do to trying harder, and you will succeed in your plan.* That is, willpower and trying harder are helpful, and all of us need to have self-control and discipline to follow through on our strategic plans. In fact, Malcolm Gladwell, the best-selling social observer, estimates that ultrasuccessful people invest ten thousand hours in their craft before they break through into world success.[2] But willpower and trying harder are not enough. Just think about your latest New Year's resolutions, where you dedicated yourself to get in shape, lose weight, stop smoking, get out of debt, or read the Bible every day. Over the course of your lifetime, how successful at keeping resolutions have you been? What is your success rate? Research by FranklinCovey indicates that we fail to keep 80 percent of our New Year's resolutions, and one-third of those don't even last until February.[3]

Yet we persist in the "I just need to work harder on my problem" mind-set. Why is that? I think it is because it helps us think, first, that we have more control in life than we do and, second, that we need less help than we do. It's uncomfortable to say that we can't do things alone and that we might have issues. "Try harder" is much simpler. The problem is, our faith comes in only when we acknowledge the futility of trying harder. We experience God's grace through Jesus' death when we are able to admit to ourselves that we can't save ourselves: "For it is by grace you have been saved, through faith—and this not from yourselves, it is the gift of God—not by works, so that no one can boast."[4] Trying harder doesn't work in connecting to God, and it doesn't work in living life either. Instead, when willpower and trying harder fail us, we are to ask for grace, guidance, and help in uncovering whatever is keeping us stuck.

So this chapter isn't a pep talk, though I hope it will encourage you. This chapter has to do with rooting out obstacles. When you deal with the seven obstacles I talk about here, you will be much freer to work your plan for solving your problem. Get these obstacles out of the way. Then allow your natural "doing right things" ability to take over.

## VALUES ISSUES

First off, your values may be askew. That is, you may not be assigning to your problem the high level of importance it warrants. When that happens, life and its demands take over, and the problem-solving plan is buried under everything else.

---

People who don't see how
important their problem is
have often not sat down and
written out their essential values.

---

My experience is that most people who don't see how important their problem is have often not sat down and intentionally written out their essential values, as I covered in Step 5. They want to be good people, and they want to be successful at something worthwhile, but they have not made the list. Business, especially in the last ten years, now names values-based decision making as a key to success, but, oddly, we don't always live like that in our personal lives.

If you were to set out your core values, you would probably find that your problem in a relationship, job, career, parenting, family, or whatever is something to pay attention to. That is, the problem may be getting in the way of love, a responsible life, or a life lived for God. So take some time to list your key values. Not making your problem a high enough priority may be a big obstacle to solving it.

## ISOLATION

A car with no gas will not leave the driveway. As I said in Step 2, you are a relational person by God's design, and that means relationships are the fuel of life. You may simply be disconnected from your needs for support, understanding, and acceptance. It is not a problem to ask for someone to listen to you and be there. It is a problem to act as if you don't need that.

And then there's the energy issue. Problems stress us out and drain a lot of energy from us, just as a cell phone uses more battery power when you are talking than when you are not. So, when you have a problem, you need more relationship, not less. Your general maintenance dosage will probably not be enough. In fact, too little relationship may be keeping you from starting your plan or staying strong on it.

When I am writing books like this one, my family and friends are always on call for a five-minute "How's it going?" conversation, so I can get their feedback on what I have written, have them be accepting of me when I am discouraged and behind schedule, or hear their excitement when they like something I've written. You and your plan can be approached the same way. In other words, look at isolation as an obstacle—and get past it.

## LACK OF STRUCTURE

I have worked with so many people using this seven-step system, people who really want to solve their problem, but they just get stuck. They do Steps 1 through 6. They have solid values, they surround themselves with great friends, and they are motivated, but they simply don't follow through. They beat themselves up and call themselves losers. Sometimes they want me to beat them up as well. But nothing gets them unstuck; nothing gets them to follow through. And this is often a problem in structure—and I don't mean structure in the sense of being personally organized. That kind of organization is a result of structure, not structure itself. Instead, I define *structure* as "the capacity to direct one's resources toward a goal over time." Structure is an ability all of us have to some degree. Three-year-olds have very little structure, so they are easily frustrated and discouraged when the toy doesn't work right. Adults are supposed to have more self-control so that they can be patient, tolerate setbacks and fatigue, and continue a project over time. But if you have structure problems, you may find yourself easily overwhelmed with life, quickly discouraged, or distracted by people or other problems.

If you find that following through on a plan doesn't work for you because you don't have enough internal structure, I assure you that trying harder will only make you feel guilty and hopeless. You need an external structure to help you develop internal structure for yourself. That is, you can't create structure inside your brain any more than you can play basketball like Kobe Bryant by tomorrow. It just won't happen.

Having a system of no-condemnation accountability with a few safe people who are for you, who are undeniably on your side, develops structure. Give your plan to them and have them check up on you at various points to encourage you. If that frequency of checking proves insufficient, have them touch base with you more often. If that isn't enough, have a consequence in place, such as if you don't get the work done this week, you have to buy someone dinner. I have done all of these to improve my own lack of structure, and they have helped me a great deal. Just make absolutely sure, though, that there is no guilt, shame, or condemnation in the relationships, or you will simply find yourself doing a better job hiding from those folks!

## FEAR

As I wrote in Step 4, fear is a paralyzer, and it needs to be vanquished. Whether you fear not doing things perfectly, making things worse, or having someone upset with you, focus on fear as an obstacle. My experience is that the more you connect your fear in relationship, the less fear you'll feel. Just as a cockroach hides from a bright light, fear does not like the light and the exposure that comes when you talk about your fear. If, for example, your problem-solving plan involves a difficult conversation with someone, role play with someone who will pretend to be that individual. You will experience the fear and anxiety, stumble through, and come out the other end seeing that you could—and will—survive that talk.

## A PASSIVE STANCE

Passivity is an attitude toward life that says, *I don't happen to life; life happens to me.* Passivity is not laziness. I know many hard-working people who can't solve life problems because they are passive inside. If you struggle with being passive, you avoid taking initiative, the first step. You generally wait for someone or something to make the first move, and you react afterward.

Sometimes passivity is rooted in the wish *If I am nice, people will be nice to me.* Sometimes the thinking is *It's selfish to ask for what I want. I hope someone will recognize my needs and meet them.* These wishes are not grounded in reality, but in childhood experiences that did not go as they should, so we get trapped in our very young thinking patterns.

The reality is that passivity will generally result in your being miserable and afraid, and will keep you from getting what you desire and need in life and love. If these words describe you, ask safe people in your life to help you become a risk taker and its first cousin, a mistake maker. Ask these people you trust to encourage you to say no, to voice your true opinions and feelings, to be more assertive, and to be more spontaneous. Exercises like these will go a long way toward helping you be a person who takes the first step.

## A PROTEST STANCE

If you find yourself arguing about the fairness of your problem, you may be stuck in a protest stance. That is another momentum-killer when it comes to solving issues.

A protest stance occurs when you can't get past the reality that you didn't cause your problem, that it resulted because of someone else or some circumstance you couldn't control. Layoffs, loss of investment value, and an unfaithful spouse all involve something outside you that you most likely had very little to do with. But often people will not even get to the Step 6 planning stage because their mind keeps returning to "It's not just!" and "It's not fair!" Sometimes a person will even think, "I won't solve the problem until the real culprit apologizes or makes restitution." And that is a recipe for a terrible life. Don't get stuck in that one.

Protest in and of itself is not a bad thing. God loves justice and hates unfairness just as you do: "You are not a God who takes pleasure in evil; with you the wicked

―――――

There is a big difference
between a protest season and
a protest identity.

―――――

cannot dwell."[5] Furthermore, protest helps us take a stand against wrongdoing, but *there is a big difference between a protest season and a protest identity.*

A protest identity happens when you can never get past whatever was unjust in your life or in the world, and you let that injustice define who you are. The antidote to the protest identity is forgiveness and grief. Only by grieving what you didn't have and forgiving those responsible can you stand against that bad thing, cancel the debt, and be free to take action steps toward solving the problem at hand.

## AN UNHEALTHY PAIN RATIO

Sometimes we don't move ahead simply because we don't have enough discomfort. That is, our situation is tolerable; we have learned to live with it and cope. Like Gumby, we have bent ourselves around a problem like we are made of rubber, and we think, "It's really not that bad." I call this an unhealthy pain ratio.

I refer to the old saying, "We change when the pain of not changing is greater than the pain of changing." This is a valuable sentence, so read it again.

While changing to avoid pain is not the highest of motivations, it is real and important. Change is work, as we have seen all the way through this book. Work involves new things, effort, discomfort, and, yes, a certain amount of pain. So I wear my shirttails out when I gain a few pounds. That is an adjustment that isn't really painful. But when I have to go to the store to buy bigger pants, that causes time, energy, and self-image pain. When we put up with a difficult marriage because we are flexible and understanding, we are adjusting and compensating. But when we look honestly at what energy it's taking, what loss of ourselves we've incurred, and what little return we get for our efforts, we change the pain ratio, come to reality, and get to work solving the problem.

If you think you may be minimizing your discomfort and living with an unhealthy pain ratio, make a list of everything that your problem is costing you. What are you spending emotionally, relationally, financially, and in personal energy to keep things the same? Also, ask some safe people what they observe about you in this regard. Their input as well as the inventory you take can be very instructive, and you may find yourself resetting your pain ratio. Yes, you may feel more pain, but that is not all bad. The pain of reality is an improvement over the anesthesia of minimization.

Once Step 6 is done, it's time to act. Clear the muck from in your head, muck that is keeping you from doing right things, and you will be amazed by your progress.

CONCLUSION:

# Now What Do You Do?

*Work out your salvation with fear and trembling;*
*for it is God who is at work in you, both to will and*
*to work for His good pleasure.*
*—Philippians 2:12-13 (NASB)*

As you finish this book, I would like to ask you to do two simple things. First, stop reading for a moment, put the book down, and, wherever you are right now, bring to mind the situation that caused you to pick up this book—the relationship problem, the money issue, the family struggle, the job problem, the health issue. You may want to look off into a corner of the room or out a window. You may want to close your eyes. But think in detail about the reality you are living in that you want to change, the present reality, the problem you face. You are bringing to mind *reality present*, what exists right now.

Having done that, now think about what you want to happen. Consider the ways you want the situation to be, not perfect and not ideal, but different, better, improved, transformed—the relationship more connected, the child happy and self-controlled, the job found. Now you are looking at reality future.

---

The only difference between reality
present and reality future always
comes down to God and you.

---

The only difference between reality present and reality future always comes down to God and you. God is here, he is for you, and he wants your best. He is moving in and working through circumstances, events, people, and your own heart, in ways both seen and unseen, to achieve his good purpose for you. And you are with him, an individual who has dreams, passions, ideas, plans, and choices, a person who can do a great deal to help create that future reality. As the verses from Philippians 2 indicate, we do our part to work out our salvation, while he does his part and works for his good pleasure. When you follow God and engage with him in the task and mission of solving significant life problems, something incredible, supernatural, and truly miraculous happens. God's power to change a dark present to a bright future activates, energizes, and adds substance to your efforts. And your path will always bear fruit, for you are walking his path with him.

God bless you.

*Dr. John Townsend*
Newport Beach, California

# ENDNOTES

## Introduction: The Problem of Having a Problem
1. John 16:33.
2. Thomas D'Zurilla and Arthur Nezu, *Problem-Solving Therapy: A Positive Approach to Clinical Intervention* (New York: Springer, 2007). An excellent approach to problem solving by two well-respected research scientists.
3. 2 Corinthians 5:19.

## Step 1: Feel What You Feel
1. John Townsend, *Leadership Beyond Reason: How Great Leaders Succeed by Harnessing the Power of Their Values, Feelings and Intuition*, chapter 3: "Emotions: The Unlikely Allies in Leadership" (Nashville: Thomas Nelson, 2009).
2. Psalm 139:23.
3. Proverbs 20:5.

## Step 2: Get with the Right People

1. Ecclesiastes 4:9–10.

2. John Townsend, *Loving People: How to Love and Be Loved* (Nashville: Thomas Nelson, 2007).

3. Henry Cloud and John Townsend, *Raising Great Kids* (Grand Rapids: Zondervan, 1999).

## Step 3: Build a Strong Fence

1. I Corinthians 14:33.

2. Galatians 6:7.

## Step 4: Break Free from Fear

1. I Peter 5:7.

## Step 5: Control What You Own

1. Proverbs 4:23.

2. Matthew 6:27.

## Step 6: Create a Pass/Fail Plan

1. Two of the best are David Allen's *Getting Things Done: The Art of Stress-Free Productivity* (New York: Penguin Books, 2001) and Dr. Henry Cloud's *The One-*

*Life Solution: Reclaiming Your Personal Life While Achieving Greater Professional Success* (New York: Collins Business, 2008).

2. Mark 4:26–29.

## Step 7: Do the Right Things

1. Genesis 1:28.
2. Malcolm Gladwell, *Outliers: The Story of Success*, chapter 2, "The 10,000 Hour Rule" (New York: Little, Brown, 2008).
3. "FranklinCovey Survey Reveals Top 3 New Year's Resolutions for 2008" (http://www.reuters.com/article/pressRelease/idUSI32935+18-Dec-2007+BW20071218).
4. Ephesians 2:8–9.
5. Psalm 5:4.

## Share Your Thoughts

**With the Author:** Your comments will be forwarded to the author when you send them to *zauthor@zondervan.com*.

**With Zondervan:** Submit your review of this book by writing to *zreview@zondervan.com*.

## Free Online Resources at
## www.zondervan.com

**Zondervan AuthorTracker:** Be notified whenever your favorite authors publish new books, go on tour, or post an update about what's happening in their lives at www.zondervan.com/authortracker.

**Daily Bible Verses and Devotions:** Enrich your life with daily Bible verses or devotions that help you start every morning focused on God. Visit www.zondervan.com/newsletters.

**Free Email Publications:** Sign up for newsletters on Christian living, academic resources, church ministry, fiction, children's resources, and more. Visit www.zondervan.com/newsletters.

**Zondervan Bible Search:** Find and compare Bible passages in a variety of translations at www.zondervanbiblesearch.com.

**Other Benefits:** Register yourself to receive online benefits like coupons and special offers, or to participate in research.

**ZONDERVAN®**

**ZONDERVAN.com/**
**AUTHORTRACKER**
*follow your favorite authors*